99.51

54|6

D1391897

WILD FLOWERS TO KNOW AND GROW

OTHER BOOKS BY JEAN HERSEY

I LIKE GARDENING

HALFWAY TO HEAVEN: A GUATEMALA HOLIDAY

GARDEN IN YOUR WINDOW

CAREFREE GARDENING

A SENSE OF SEASONS

WILD FLOWERS
to Know
and Grow

by Jean Hersey

Paintings by Allinora Rosse

D. VAN NOSTRAND COMPANY, INC.

Princeton, New Jersey
Toronto
New York
London

99157

635. 9676

D. VAN NOSTRAND COMPANY, INC.
120 Alexander St., Princeton, New Jersey (*Principal office*)
24 West 40 Street, New York 18, New York

D. VAN NOSTRAND COMPANY, LTD.
358, Kensington High Street, London, W.14, England

D. VAN NOSTRAND COMPANY (Canada), LTD.
25 Hollinger Road, Toronto 16, Canada

Published simultaneously in Canada by
D. VAN NOSTRAND COMPANY (Canada), LTD.

To the memory of
LILLIAN WADSWORTH
whose appreciation of Nature
has been an inspiration to me through the years

Prologue: WILD FLOWERS—
MY FIRST AWARENESS

One enchanted summer a number of years ago my husband and I camped our way across the country. On a certain day, driving through the Rockies, we rounded a bend and a whole mountainside of flowers lay before us! You could not see the earth so thick were the blossoms. We stopped, walked among them, sat in them, and revelled in their sweeps of pink and white, and their delicate fragrance. That moment awakened in me a love of wild flowers that will never diminish. We now live in a meadow in Connecticut surrounded by more than a hundred varieties of native plants. What that Colorado mountainside initiated, our own meadow carried on. We both have become ardent wild-flower enthusiasts.

You may not be able to view the mountain slopes of blue Lupine along the California coast, or to visit Kansas when miles of sunflowers are in bloom. You may never see the blossoming of the Mojave Desert in spring, the wild Trillium in Ohio, or, in autumn, the Goldenrod fringing Cape Cod beaches. But no matter. In your own garden, small or large, you can grow such a multitude of native plants that you capture the spirit of the floral beauty that is our national heritage, and live with it day by day, and through all seasons.

Though I never discovered the names of those Rocky Mountain flowers, they led me into this lovely new world that grows more thrilling every year—a world that I want to share with you.

JEAN HERSEY

Weston, Connecticut
January, 1964

Acknowledgments

In developing this book, I have been helped by many people. First of all, my deepest thanks and appreciation go to Helen Van Pelt Wilson who, from beginning to end, has been far more than friend and editor. Her enthusiasm and encouragement all the way have been invaluable.

I am particularly grateful to Allianora Rosse who has captured the beauty and excitement of wild gardening in her handsome color illustrations; to George Taloumis who made several long trips to photograph our native plants, and so successfully caught the feel of the land; to Mrs. Fred J. Hay for her appealing arrangement picture taken especially for this book; to Mrs. Alice Harvey Hubbard for her help with the chapters on Conservation; to Henry B. Van Sinderen for information shared at lunch one day; and to P. L. Ricker, president of the Wild Flower Preservation Society.

I would also like especially to thank my secretary, Mrs. June Schlegel, for her interest and tireless cooperation that carried well beyond the call of duty.

Appreciation is likewise expressed to editors for permission to reprint material that has appeared in their publications: *Woman's Day Magazine,* a Fawcett Publication; *Flower Grower, The Home Garden Magazine; Flower and Garden; Horticulture; The American Home;* and *The New York Times* Garden Section.

I should also like to thank G. P. Putnam's Sons for permission to reprint the quotation from Wilhelm Miller that appeared in *My Wild Flower Garden* by Herbert Durand (1927).

CONTENTS

Part I
Wild Flowers to Know

Part II
Wild Flowers to Grow

Part III
Wild Flowers to Protect

Our house is set in a field of yellow-and-orange hawkweed, black-eyed Susans, and daisies. Wild iris, Canada lilies, and golden alexanders are among the hundred different varieties of wild flowers that thrive along our walls and stream, and in the meadow. (George Taloumis Photo)

Indian Poke, Skunk Cabbage, Cardinal Flower, Wild Calla, and Watercress grow along our brook. In April, Marsh Marigolds turn the area gold. These sometimes float downstream and appear in new places next year. (George Taloumis Photo)

On our land a variety of ferns, jewelweed, violets, Wakerobin, as well as Skunk Cabbage and Indian Poke, bring contrasting foliage and flowers to this wooded area with its backdrop of a fallen log. (George Taloumis Photo)

In June, false Solomon's-Seal is a sweep of white blossoms along our hundred-year-old gray stone walls. In fall, the interesting ribbed foliage turns translucent gold in striking contrast to the nearby scarlet swamp maples. (George Taloumis Photo)

Along our primrose path royal ferns raise feathery fronds. They sparkle in rain, and in sunlight their shadows dance over the leafy woodland floor. (George Taloumis Photo)

The saw-edged, triple leaves of toothwort offer a background for the delicate white flowers that open in May. These white drifts enhance the shady woodland paths that fringe our stream. (George Taloumis Photo)

Beach grass, seaside goldenrod, and Artemisia grow with abandon along the shore of Cape Cod. Bring a touch of sea and salt to your land by growing some of these if your soil and location are right. (George Taloumis Photo)

Wild meadow flowers lend themselves to exquisite indoor bouquets. Mrs. Fred J. Hay of South Carolina gathered these from her own land and arranged them in a Cherokee Indian basket. This bouquet includes: Queen Anne's lace, goldenrod, Cardinal Flower, white Snakeroot, wild Sunflower, black-eyed Susans, tall flat-top white Asters, and pearly Everlasting (in bud). Edward L. DuPuy Photo)

Part I

WILD FLOWERS TO KNOW

Speak to the earth, and it shall teach thee.
—Job 12:8

1. Discover a Wonderful New World

On a fine summer day you turn off the highway and pause to eat lunch in a meadow beside a meandering stream. How curious are those blue flowers at the water's edge. And what is this shiny-leaved, creeping yellow flower in the grass? That sweep of gold in the open field that bends and flows like a river with each puff of breeze?

Flowers are like people. When you don't know a man's name or anything about him, you usually have only a passing interest in him. But once you learn the stranger's name, where he lives, and a little about what he likes, you feel you have made a new friend—you greet him warmly next time you meet.

Similarly, you establish rapport with an unfamiliar flower when you learn its name, something about how it grows, and where it comes from. When you meet this flower again, in another location, it fairly leaps to greet you. If you learn that the blue flower by the water is Blue Flag, or Fleur-de-Lis, immediately you regard it differently. Next time you pause by a sunny meadow stream in June, you hunt for it. Catching sight of the charming blue blossoms unfurling in the midst of lancelike foliage, so Japanese in appearance, you greet your old friend. How much fun to have suspected it might grow there, and to have guessed correctly!

Begin identifying wild flowers and you rapidly run into the fun of names that may be amusing (Blue Curls), intriguing (Butter-and-Eggs), mysterious (Loosestrife), repulsive (Lousewort), romantic (False Dragonhead), gay (Butterfly Weed), or sinister (Vipers' Bugloss). They can be anything, including long and Latin, but they are never dull!

THEY'RE EVERYWHERE

And what a great range of locations wild flowers thrive in! Observe how the same flower flourishes in a number of different areas, and varies in each. Fringed Gentian growing in dry and gravelly soil is dark in color, short and small as to bloom, while the flowers of a Fringed Gentian that grows in grass near a damp ditch will be paler, but larger and more deeply fringed.

In early spring most of the first flowers are found in the woods. Here they bloom in sunlight filtered through the trees' still-leafless branches. The foliage of these early kinds often flourishes and fades well ahead of other green-

4

ery. The majority of the late summer and fall flowers are apt to be found in open fields and along roadsides.

Wherever you go, carry a small notebook. If a flower you have just identified is new to you, if it especially appeals, draw a simple sketch of the blossom so you will remember it, and also of the leaf, at times a leaf is equally helpful in identification. A sketch is especially important when you cannot pick the flower because it wilts rapidly or is protected by conservation laws. In some cases, picking the blooms prevents a plant from flowering again and it soon dies (as the Lady's-Slipper and Cardinal Flower). In Chapter 2, you will find notes as to the flowers you may and may not pick, and a partial conservation list in Chapter 16.

Of course, a camera, equipped for close-up pictures, is an excellent substitute for a sketchbook, but you will still need pad and pencil for recording pertinent information about the plant: its environment, the date and time of day of your observation, and so on.

In addition to your notebook, a pocket magnifying glass is useful. It will open up a new world of beauty for you within each flower. More important, it will permit you to really *see* the minute flower parts, which may be the only means of differentiating two flowers similar in outward appearance.

5

WILD FLOWERS TO KNOW

The World . . . and Beyond

At any season of the year, in woods and meadows, there is a world within a world for those who tread softly and look carefully. There is something about appreciating small things, tiny flowers and such, that makes you feel you should tiptoe and be quiet. And when you are quiet, you also hear small sounds that otherwise you might miss: a beetle crawling across a leaf, perhaps, and then you have a new respect for his path, his way, and an interest in where he is going. You hear the plop of a frog in the stream, the breeze through stiff grass, and the tiniest sound of all, the Jewelweed snapping open its pods to spread seed. We are told there are sounds our human ears are not equipped to hear, but we can still stretch our listening to include a number of sounds that we are equipped to hear, but often miss in the hurry and bustle of living.

So your interest in wild flowers soon becomes a way to increased awareness. To be aware is to be receptive, and soon other senses are involved.

You also become alert to subtle scents everywhere—the smell of a field with the sun on it, or of deep woods with a floor of wet oak leaves. How different is the fragrance of each.

Sharpening and developing the sense of touch among

6

wild flowers opens up yet another door. Run your hand up the delicate, feathery foliage of Wild Carrot, feel the smooth shiny leaf of a Marsh Marigold. What a difference. What a difference between the firm vigor of a wild Iris spear and the feathery brush of Hawkweed's stems as you walk through a June meadow.

As you make friends with wild flowers and learn their names, as you experience the joys of their fragrance, the feel of them, the beauty of their color, of their line and form, your private world stretches to include the larger world of nature. And by achieving this, you are stirred to reverence for the basic plan of things. Wild flowers and their ways tell you a great deal that is new and exciting, if you listen, and look, and smell, and feel—if you are curious, and if you wonder.

2. Two Hundred Wild Flowers
to Know

When you see a wild flower you don't recognize, first ask yourself two questions about it: What color is it? What season is it blooming? Color and time of blooming are the easiest means to identification and the main bases for identification in this book.

The two hundred wild flowers pictured and described in this chapter are arranged by color into four groups:

1. White, Variable and Off-White, Green Tints
2. Clear Blue, Lavender, and Purple
3. Yellow, Orange-Yellow, and Orange
4. Pink, Purple-Red, and Red

You will discover that flower tints vary from bloom to bloom within a species and that soil and season also affect the shading of a flower. Butterfly Weed may be light yellow in one place and orange to almost red in another. Wild Geranium goes from a light pink-lavender to quite deep purple. Beardtongue or Penstemon is white, pink-white, occasionally light blue. Still, the variations almost always occur within only one of our four groups.

And within the color groups, the wild flowers are ordered by time of blooming. Look for a blue flower you come upon in early spring at the beginning of the second color group, an orange-yellow in September, toward the end of the third color group. Of course, many plants bloom almost at the same time, so the order must be somewhat arbitrary, but still you will find close together in one group, say, the blue flowers of spring.

We have used these convenient seasonal divisions: Spring: March, April, May; Summer: June, July, August; Fall: September, October, November.

In addition to these two hundred paintings of wild flowers, you will find the notes on geographical distribution and habitat helpful in identification. Some species like Flaming Sword occur in Arizona, California, and New Mexico; and the Western Bleeding Heart favors the Yosemite Valley. Trailing Arbutus belongs to the East. If, in early spring, you find a yellow flower in a bog or beside a stream, it could be a Marsh Marigold. It would hardly be a golden Sundrop, which might well appear in your meadow, however.

The notes "may pick" and "don't pick" have two purposes: to prevent your taking flowers from plants like the

Lady's-Slipper or Trillium that die if their blooms are picked; to help you avoid the disappointment of cutting for bouquets flowers that are poor "keepers," like the Butterfly Weed or Wood Anemone. In some cases, both reasons apply—the plants die and, furthermore, the flowers immediately wilt.

Some flowers and plants are protected by a state conservation law; a great many are on the conservation lists of garden clubs, whose members are making strenuous and worthwhile efforts to prevent the disappearance of many lovely wildlings. Lists vary from one locality to another, but certain plants appear on almost every list and we have pointed out some of these in Chapter 16.

As you become familiar with the flowers in these lovely paintings by Allianora Rosse, your awareness of the many wild flowers close by will be increased. We hope you will enjoy studying the pictures in wintertime and using them for identification through the growing seasons of spring, summer, and fall.

WHITE, VARIABLE AND OFF-WHITE, GREEN TINTS

PLATE 1

1. Bearberry—*Arctostaphylos uva-ursi*. White. 6 ins. Carpets Cape Cod's rolling Truro hills with mats, thick and bouncy to walk on. Red fall berries are decorative. Delicate bell-shaped flowers open in spring. At the fringes of oak and pine woodlands, dry meadows, roadsides. Acid sandy soil. Don't pick.

2. Bloodroot—*Sanguinaria canadensis*. White. 10 ins. Juice of root and stem red. Cylinder-shaped leaf encloses budding flower. Petals flat in morning, erect at noon, closed at dusk. Blooms spring. Grows in dry, high or low woodland, at shady brookside. Neutral soil. Don't pick, for the flowers soon wither and the plant is harmed.

3. Dutchman's-Breeches—*Dicentra cucullaria*. White, tipped with gold. 5-9 ins. Nodding flowers on tawny, arching stalk. The two-spurred blossom resembles Dutch pantaloons. Grows in stony, high or low woodlands, along shady brooks. Feathery, fernlike foliage introduces spring. Acid or neutral soil. Don't pick.

4. False Solomon's-Seal—*Smilacina racemosa*. White. 1-3 ft. Clustered blossoms look like lace. Alternate green, wavy-edged leaves. Ruby red berries in fall when its leaves turn gold. Blooms spring, in high and low woodland. Acid soil. Don't pick.

5. Foamflower—*Tiarella cordifolia*. White. 6-12 ins. Feathery spike of snowy flowers. Bronze leaves by fall. Low woodland and shady brookside. Blooms spring. Acid to neutral soil. Don't pick.

6. Large Flowering Trillium—*Trillium grandiflorum*. White. 7-15 ins. Grows wild by the acre in wooded areas, I think of one outside Cleveland, Ohio. Spring blooms. Acid to neutral soil. Don't pick.

1

2

3

4

5

6

PLATE 2

7. Solomon's-Seal—*Polygonatum biflorum.* White. 1-3 ft. Delicate twin blossoms on arching stalk beneath each leaf. Berries blue-black in fall. Spring flowering. High dry woodland, along stone walls. Acid to neutral soil. Don't pick.

8. Sweet White Violet—*Viola blanda.* White. 3-5 ins. Tender heart-shaped leaves are good in salad. Blooms early in spring. Low woodlands, brookside, sunny wet pastures. May pick.

9. Toothwort, Crinkleroot—*Dentaria diphylla.* White. 8-13 ins. Long root has Watercress flavor. Leaves are three-lobed and notched. Spring. Shady brookside and sunny bogs. Acid soil. Don't pick.

10. Wild Lily-of-the-Valley—*Maianthemum canadense.* White. 3-6 ins. Feathery flowers, shiny leaves, red fall berries. Blooms in the spring at shady brookside. Acid soil. Don't pick.

11. Wood Anemone, Wind Flower—*Anemone quinquefolia.* White. 6-12 ins. Flower on a single stalk rises above wet winter leaves in spring. Grows in high and low woodland, at brookside. Acid soil. Don't pick.

12. Yarrow, Milfoil—*Achillea Millefolium.* White. 1-2 ft. Grows from coast to coast. Feathery foliage, aromatic. Flat head of tiny flowers bewitching when magnified. Flowers early summer, in dry meadows or woodland, in poor soil. May pick.

13. Bunchberry—*Cornus canadensis.* White. 3-8 ins. Dogwood family. Compact bunches of scarlet berries in August. Flowers spring and summer in woodland and at brookside. Acid soil. Don't pick.

7

8

9

10

11

12

13

PLATE 3

14. Field Chickweed—*Cerastium arvense*. White. 4-10 ins. A handsome, deeply cleft version of Common Chickweed. Flowers in early summer. Hot, dry pastures with acid soil. May pick.

15. Goldthread—*Coptis trifolia*. White. 3-6 ins. Miniature flower; shiny, deckle-edged green leaves. Named for its roots like yellow threads. Flowers in early summer in low woodland and at shady brookside. Acid soil. Don't pick.

16. Groundnut, Dwarf Ginseng—*Panax trifolium*. White. 3-6 ins. Heads of flowers top a stalk above the leaves. The second name is from the Chinese *Jin-Chen* or "man-like" because of its two-legged root. Early summer flowers in low woodland and at brookside. Acid to neutral soil. May pick.

17. Indian Poke, False or American White Hellebore—*Veratrum viride*. Yellow-green. 2-7 ft. Beautifully lined, light-green young leaves appear pleated. Roots and leaves poisonous. Insignificant flowers in early summer. Grows along stream banks and in sunny bogs. Acid soil. Don't pick.

18. Marsh Trefoil, Buck Bean—*Menyanthes trifoliata*. White. 10 ins. A snowflake ensnared in a flower! Wavy petals open to reveal miniature feathers and brown stamens. Blooms, early summer, in sunny bogs. Acid soil. Don't pick.

19. New Jersey Tea—*Ceanothus americanus*. White. 1-4 ft. Fragrant, plumy flower clusters. Soldiers in the American Revolution brewed its leaves for tea. Flowers spring and summer in high, dry woodland, along stone walls. Acid to neutral soil. May pick.

PLATE 4

20. Partridgeberry, Twinberry—*Mitchella repens*. Pinkish-white. 6-12. ins., trailing. Starry flowers, glossy leaves, and red berries. Blooms in early summer. Grows in dry woodlands in an acid soil. Don't pick.

21. Red Baneberry—*Actaea rubra*. White. 1-2 ft. Soft flowers in clusters on slender stem. Coral fruit (poisonous) in fall. Blooms spring, summer, in high, dry woodlands. Acid to neutral soil. May pick.

22. Starflower—*Trientalis borealis*. White. 3-7 ins. Delicate flowers with orange anthers rise above a medieval ruff of lance-shaped leaves. Blooms spring, summer, along shady brooks and at fringes of woodland. Acid soil. Don't pick.

23. Western Evening Primrose—*Anogra albicaulis*. White. 2 ft. The flowers, like single roses, carpet western prairies. Blooms spring, summer, in hot, dry open meadows. Don't pick.

24. Wood Sorrel—*Oxalis acetosella*. White, pink-veined. 3-4 ins. Three light-green, heart-shaped leaflets fold together at night. Frail flowers in spring, summer. Grows at edge of brooks and in woodlands. Don't pick.

25. Yucca, Spanish Bayonet, Our Lord's Candle—*Hespero-Yucca whipplei*. White. 5-15 ft. State Flower of New Mexico. Huge shafts of blossoms rise from blue-green, dagger-like foliage. They stand like giant candles on rugged western mountain slopes. Blooms in summer in hot, dry, gravelly meadows. Adam's-Needle, *Yucca filamentosa,* common in the East, blooms late spring or early summer. Don't pick.

20

21

22

23   24   25

PLATE 5

26. American Lotus, Sacred Bean—*Nelumbo lutea.* White with gold centers. Grows in 2-6 ft. of water. Leaves are 1-2 ft. broad. Found in ponds; flowers rise above surface. Its tubers were a favorite food of the Indians, hence the second name, Sacred Bean. Seed pods as dramatic as its flowers. Blooms in summer. May pick.

27. Beach Clotbur—*Xanthium echinatum.* Greenish. 1-2 ft. Green spiny burrs found on beaches, bluffs, and dunes. Burr sticks to clothing and thus travels to new growing area. Prospers in sandy, gravelly waste areas and dry meadows. Don't pick.

28. Beardtongue, Penstemon—*Penstemon hirsutus.* White. 2 ft. Easy to transplant to your own yard. Soak soil around plant a few days after moving. Blooms in summer in sunny meadows and woodland fringes. May pick.

29. Bladder Campion, White Vein—*Silene latifolia.* White. 6-20 ins. Native of Europe, naturalized here. Petals (5) with red-brown anthers (10) emerge from melon-shaped cup whose markings suggest a miniature cantaloupe! Blooms in summer in dry pastures and sunny wet meadows. May pick.

30. Buttonbush, Bushglobe Flower—*Cephalanthus occidentalis.* White. 3-10 ft. Delightfully fragrant flowers resemble round cushions stuck with hundreds of white pins. Found in summer in swamps and on low ground along lake shores, all across the country. May pick.

31. Hedge Bindweed—*Convolvulus sepium.* White, pink-tinted. 3-10 ft., trailing. Arrow-shaped gray-green leaves. Handsome, bell-like flowers resemble new tissue paper. Open in morning, closed by noon. Grows in sunny, moist areas. Don't pick.

26

27

28

29

30

31

PLATE 6

32. Indian Pipe—*Monotropa uniflora*. White. 3-9 ins. Weird, ghostly flower with waxy bloom suggests an upside down meerschaum pipe. Flowers in summer in deep woods, pine or oak. Collapses in sunlight. Acid soil. Don't pick.

33. Lizard-Tail—*Saururus cernuus*. White. 2-5 ft. Heart-shaped leaves. Fragrant flower spike droops in a curve at the top. Blossoms soft and pleasant to touch. Cut, long-lasting indoors. Blooms in summer on streambanks and in wet meadows. May pick.

34. May Apple, Wild Mandrake—*Podophyllum peltatum*. White. 12-18 ins. Single yellow-centered flowers open beneath shiny umbrella-like leaves. Lemon-shaped, edible berries follow. Leaves and roots poisonous. Blooms in summer in wet pastures and woodlands. Soil acid to neutral. Don't pick.

35. Oxeye-Daisy, Common White Daisy—*Chrysanthemum leucanthemum*. White. 15-24 ins. Native of Europe. Flowers in summer everywhere in the country. Subject of poem and song. The stuff of which daisy chains are made; find out if "he loves you or loves you not." Do pick.

36. Pipsissewa, Prince's Pine—*Chimaphila umbellata*. Creamy white. 6-12 ins. Evergreen shiny leaves are sharply toothed, the undersides often reddish. Fragrant waxy flowers enchanting. Blooms in summer in high and low woodlands. Acid soil. Don't pick.

37. Rattlesnake Plantain—*Epipactis tesselata*. Greenish white. 5-8 ins. Hardy orchid. Grows under hemlock and spruce on north side of stone walls. Gray-green leaves, each marked with pale-green pencilling. Acid soil. Don't pick.

32

33

34

35

36

37

PLATE 7

38. Round-leaved Sundew—*Drosera rotundifolia.* White. 4-9 ins. Carnivorous. Sticky, hairy basal leaves attract insects. Hairs curl around stuck-fast prey, and plant then absorbs it. Colorful sap stains paper a deep purple. Blooms in summer in low woodland and wet meadows. Don't pick.

39. Sweet-Scented Bedstraw—*Galium triflorum.* White. 1-3 ft., trailing. Dry its foliage for lasting fragrance. Said to have lined the Christ-child's manger. Blooms in summer in high and low woodlands. May pick.

40. Tall Meadow Rue—*Thalictrum polygamum.* White. 3-6 ft. Blue-green foliage similar to that of Columbine. Clusters of frost-like patterned flowers in bloom in summer in damp meadows. For special enjoyment, magnify. May pick.

41. Thimbleweed, Tall Anemone—*Anemone virginiana.* Greenish-white. 2-3 ft. Deep olive green with slightly hairy leaves. Seed pod resembles thimble. Blooms in summer in high woodland and along stone walls. Acid to neutral soil. Don't pick.

42. Virgin's-Bower, Clematis—*Clematis virginiana.* White. Climbing to 15 ft. Drapes snowy flower clusters and coarse leaves over bushes and walls. Sometimes called Old Man's Beard, because of hoary appearance of silver-green seed pods. Blooms in sunny summer meadows and wet fields. Acid to neutral soil. May pick.

43. Washington Lily, Shasta Lily—*Lilium washingtonianum.* White. 2-5 ft. Sweet-spicy blooms grow in clusters, two to twenty flowers on a stalk. A dramatic sight in western foothills, Yosemite, and Columbia River areas. Blooms in summer. High shaded woodland and forest fringes, moist places. Acid to neutral soil. May pick.

38

39

40

41

42

43

PLATE 8

44. Water Hemlock, Spotted Cowbane—*Cicuta maculata.* White. 3-6 ft. Flowers in loose clusters branching from a dull magenta-marked stem. Especially beautiful magnified. Roots contain a deadly alkaloid. From the same family as the Hemlock used by the ancient Greeks to execute enemies. Flowers in summer in damp fields. May pick.

45. Wild Calla, Water Arum—*Calla palustris.* White. 5-10 ins. Attractive heart-shaped leaves. Yellow finger-like spadix covered with florets. Fertilized by pond snails. Clustered red berries ripen in August. Blooms in summer in sunny, wet meadows and along streams. Don't pick.

46. Wintergreen, Checkerberry—*Gaultheria procumbens.* White. 2-5 ins. Glossy leaves, urn-shaped waxy flowers. Red berries beloved of small boys for wintergreen flavor. Blooms in summer. High dry woodland. Acid soil. Don't pick.

47. Climbing Wild Cucumber, Wild Balsam Apple—*Echinocystis lobata.* Greenish white. 15-20 ft., climbing. From the Greek meaning "hedgehog," alluding to the 2-inch fruits armed with spines. Appealing spiral tendrils. Fragrant blooms in summer. Brookside or bog. Don't pick.

48. Culver's Root—*Veronicastrum virginicum.* White. 2-7 ft. Flowers at top of stalk bend like kittens' tails. Blooms in summer in meadows and woodlands. May pick.

49. Daisy Fleabane—*Erigeron ramosus.* White. 1-2 ft. Small yellow-centered daisies borne on branching flower stems. Like Baby's-Breath. Lovely in bouquets. Blooms in summer in dry sunny meadows and poor, gravelly soil. May pick.

44

45

46

47

48

49

PLATE 9

50. Datura, Thorn Apple, Jimson Weed—*Datura stramonium*. White. 1-5 ft. Naturalized from Asia. Fragrant trumpet-shaped, 4-in. flowers. Note enchanting fat, round, spiny seed pod with smooth ruff around its neck. Flowers in summer in sunny meadows and waste places. Poisonous if eaten. May pick.

51. Evening Lychnis, White Campion—*Lychnis alba*. White. 1-2 ft. Naturalized from Europe. Oval vase-shaped cup with maroon markings. Slightly sticky. Fragrant flowers, oval leaves with gracefully curling points. Blooms in summer, and fall, in sunny meadows. May pick.

52. Pearly Everlasting, Moonshine—*Anaphalis margaritacea*. White. 1-3 ft. Sage green leaves, snowy crisp-petaled flowers with tawny yellow centers. Hang upside down to dry for winter bouquets. Blooms in summer, fall, in open meadows. May pick.

53. Queen Anne's Lace, Wild Carrot—*Daucus carota*. White. 2-3 ft. Flower heads enhance all bouquets. For special enjoyment, magnify. Goes to seed like a bunch of wool in a brown bird cage. Often called Bird's-Nest. Blooms summer and fall in dry meadows and woodland fringes. Do pick.

54. Rattlesnake Root, White Lettuce—*Prenanthes alba*. White. 2-4 ft. Leaves suggest oak-leaf lettuce, toothed and cut. Windblown flowers on branching stalks. Fragrant blooms open summer, fall, at edge of woodland. May pick.

55. Slender Ladies'-Tresses—*Spiranthes gracilis*. Cream white. 10-22 ins. Sweetly fragrant, tiny flowers twisting up a stalk suggest braid of hair. Bloom in summer in sunny meadow and woodland's fringe. Don't pick.

50

51

52

53

54

55

PLATE 10

56. Turtlehead—*Chelone glabra*. Pinkish-white, pink. 1-2 ft. Fragrant blossom resembles a turtle's head with open mouth. Blooms summer, fall, persisting even after frost. Low woodlands. Don't pick.

57. White Thoroughwort—*Eupatorium album*. White. 1-3 ft. Fragrant downy flowers grow in heads at top of leaf stalk. Resembles garden Ageratum and is often called Perennial Ageratum. Blooms summer in high and low woodland, fringe of shade. May pick.

58. White Water Lily—*Nymphaea odorata*. White flowers, 4-9 ins. across. Waxy gold-centered flowers float on water amid glossy green leaves. Blooms summer, fall all across the country. Don't pick.

59. Wild Mint—*Mentha arvensis*. White, pale lavender. 1-2 ft. Furry flowers, arranged in clusters, circle plant stem at joint of leaves. Leaves delicious in fruit drinks. Blooms in summer, fall, in sun or shade, wet and dry areas. May pick.

60. Michaelmas Daisy, Heath Aster—*Aster ericoides*. White. 1-3 ft. Blooms along roadsides and meadows in fall, defying frost. In October and November, fringes the purple Cape Cod cranberry bogs. May pick.

61. Sharp-Leaf Wood Aster—*Aster acuminatus*. Lilac-white. 10-16 ins. Coarse-toothed dark green leaves arranged in a near-circle beneath long-stemmed fragrant flowers. Autumn in high, dry woodlands, roadsides, meadows. Acid soil. May pick.

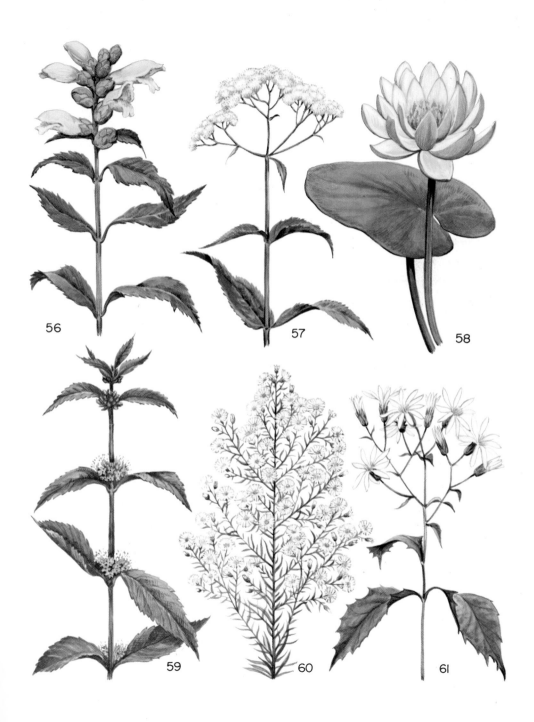

56   57   58

59   60   61

CLEAR BLUE, LAVENDER, AND PURPLE

PLATE 11

62. Bird's-foot Violet—*Viola pedata*. Light violet. 4-10 ins. State Flower of Wisconsin. Also grows on Nantucket and the Massachusetts shore. Leaves cut, slashed, toothed. Dot of orange or yellow in center of flower. Blooms in spring at edge of woodland and in sandy, sunny areas. Don't pick.

63. Common Violet—*Viola cucullata*. Light purple. 3-7 ins. State Flower of Rhode Island, New Jersey, and Illinois. Said to have been Napoleon's favorite flower. Delicious candied. Lovely to eat, to wear, to look at. Found everywhere in spring. May pick.

64. Crested Dwarf Iris—*Iris cristata*. Lavender-blue. 1-3 ins. Flowers have yellow and white crest. Grows in the mountains of North Carolina and California. Blooms, spring, in sandy loam and humus, in woodland areas. May pick.

65. Forget-me-not—*Myosotis scorpioides*. Light blue. 6-15 ins. A native of Asia and Europe, it now thrives along our streams. Dainty blossoms last days in old-fashioned bouquets. Blooms spring, summer, and fall in sunny or damp fields. May pick.

66. Hepatica, Liverleaf—*Hepatica triloba*. Blue, pink, lilac, white. 3-5 ins. Blossoms emerge among the first in spring. Furry-stemmed blooms touched with white. Thrives in high and low woodland in slightly acid to neutral soil. Don't pick.

67. Jack-in-the-Pulpit, Indian Turnip—*Arisaema triphyllum*. Purple, brown, green. 1-2 ft. Striped hood arches over erect stalk of tiny true flowers between a pair of triple leaves. Handsome berry-like fruit is scarlet in late summer. Blooms springtime in woodlands. Don't pick.

62

63

64

65

66

67

PLATE 12

68. Pasqueflower—*Anemone patent*. Pale violet. 6-14 ins. State Flower of South Dakota. A silky, furry plant growing on western mountain slopes, prairies, high meadows. Blooms arrive before spring snows have melted, warmed by their gray "fur." Don't pick.

69. Skunk Cabbage—*Symplocarpus foetidus*. Dark purple, red, green. Flowers, 1 ft.; leaves, 2 ft. Wonderfully curling, swirling rhythm in shell-like flower sheath. Smells more like raw onion and mustard than skunk. Blooms, spring, in shady or sunny bogs. May pick.

70. Virginia Cowslip, Bluebells—*Mertensia virginica*. Light blue. 1-2 ft. Nodding pink buds open to light blue flowers. A member of the Borage Family. Flowers in the spring, in woodlands, along streambanks. Acid to neutral soil. Don't pick.

71. Wild Ginger—*Asarum canadense*. Brown-purple. 6-12 ins. Small juglike blossom hides under woolly, heart-shaped leaves. Among the earliest spring flowers. Grows in high, dry woodlands and creeps over rocky boulders. Acid soil. Don't pick.

72. Red Clover—*Trifolium pratense*. Dusty magenta. 8-24 ins. State Flower of Vermont. Introduced into Australia, unsuccessfully until American bees were also introduced. First blossoms appear early. Sunny meadows, roadsides. Fragrant. May pick.

73. Bluets, Quaker-Ladies, Innocence—*Houstonia caerulea*. Blue. 3-6 ins. Charming blue petals surround snowy white center. Foliage like hay. Blooms spring, summer, in sunny meadows. May pick.

68

69

70

71

72

73

PLATE 13

74. Blue-eyed Grass—*Sisyrinchium angustifolium.* Deep violet blue. 6-13 ins. In the heart of the blue flower is a white star accented gold. Each petal tipped with thornlike point. Blooms spring, summer. Sunny fields, wet pastures. Don't pick.

75. Jacob's-Ladder—*Polemonium vanbruntiae.* Violet. 8-12 ins. Ladder-like arrangement of leaves. Violet bell-shaped flowers with white thread-like parts. Blooms spring, summer, at edge of woodland. Don't pick.

76. Large Blue Flag, Fleur-de-Lis—*Iris versicolor.* Violet blue. 16-30 ins. Iris is the Greek term for rainbow. Deep navy blue, furled buds as lovely as open flower. Each blossom lasts a day, but many appear. Blooms spring, summer. Wet meadows. May pick.

77. Leather Flower—*Clematis ochroleuca.* Pale lavender. 1-2 ft. Hairy, silky stems with nodding flowers. Yellowish-brown, shaggy seed pod equally attractive. Blooms spring, summer. High woodlands, sunny meadows. Don't pick.

78. Robin's-Plantain—*Erigeron pulchellus.* Lilac. 10-22 ins. Gold-centered, daisy-like flowers, soft hairy leaves and stems. Thrives in gravelly, dry spots as well as sunny meadows. Blooms spring, summer. May pick.

79. Sego Lily, Mariposa Tulip—*Calochortus nuttalli.* Pale lilac and white. 12 ins. State Flower of Utah. Petals delicately fluted. Grows on Bright Angel Trail at Grand Canyon and throughout Southwest. Revered by Mormons, since its bulb was important in the diet of early Mormon pioneers while crossing the desert. Blooms spring, summer. Hot dry areas. May pick.

74

75

76

77

78

79

PLATE 14

80. Selfheal, Heal-All—*Prunella vulgaris.*   Purple. 6-13 ins. Flowers constantly guarded by bees and yellow butterflies seeking nectar. Used by the old-fashioned country housewife in herbal brews for medicine. Blooms spring, summer, everywhere. May pick.

81. Spiderwort—*Tradescantia virginiana.*   Ultramarine blue. 1-3 ft. Named for a favorite gardener of King Charles I, John Tradescant. New blooms open daily and are fertilized by bees. Blooms spring and summer everywhere. Do pick.

82. Wild Blue Phlox—*Phlox divaricata.*   Lavender. 9-18 ins. Heads of bloom carpet thinly wooded areas, sending a sweet meadow fragrance far and wide. Blooms spring, summer. Acid to neutral soil. Do pick.

83—Wild Geranium, Cranesbill—*Geranium maculatum.*   Rose-lavender. 1-2 ft. Deeply-cut leaves are soft and hairy. Anthers often peacock blue. Fertilized by honeybees. Blooms spring and summer, in low woodlands and by roadsides. Acid to neutral soil. Don't pick.

84. American Brookline, Speedwell—*Veronica americana.*   Brilliant blue. 6-15 ins. Stem creeps, then stands erect and produces at its tip flowers tiny as the Forget-me-nots. Blooms spring, summer. Woodland, brookside. Don't pick.

85. Bellflower—*Campanula rapunculoides.* Purple. 2-3 ft. Bell-shaped flowers grow on one side of the stem. Lowest blossoms open first. Hairy leaves. Blooms, summer, in dry pastures and fringe of woodland. Do pick.

80

81

82

83

84

85

PLATE 15

86. Blunt-leaved Milkweed—*Asclepias amplexicaulis.* Lilac. 2-3 ft. Leaves ruffled and wavy; pods long and slim, shaped like a heron. Blooms, summer, in sunny meadows and at roadsides. Don't pick.

87. Common Milkweed—*Asclepian syriaca.* Lilac. 3-5 ft. Clusters of florets brown outside, lavender within. Deeply fragrant. Rough pod bursts into loose downy parachutes, each bearing a seed. Blooms summer everywhere. Do pick.

88. False Dragonhead, Lion's-Heart—*Physostegia virginiana.* Lilac. 1-4 ft. Blossoms, like little tubes flaring at ends, cluster at top of stem. Blooms summer. Thrives shady brookside, sunny bog. May pick.

89. Heartleaf Twayblade—*Listera cordata.* Dull purple. 3-10 ins. Small flower emerges from pair of heart-shaped leaves. Grows in woods from Vermont to Oregon. Flower ejects a sticky substance; thus, pollen clings to insects and is transported. Blooms, summer, in low woodlands. Acid soil. Don't pick.

90. Large Purple-fringed orchis—*Habenaria fimbriata.* Purple. 12-30 ins. Fragrant flower spike beloved of butterflies and bees. Blooms in summer in wet pastures. Don't pick.

91. Larkspur—*Delphinium tricorne.* Deep blue or white. 3 ft. Name from the Greek word for "dolphin," as the bud resembles a dolphin tossing on the sea. Blooms, summer, in high, dry woodland and sunny meadows. Acid to neutral soil. May pick.

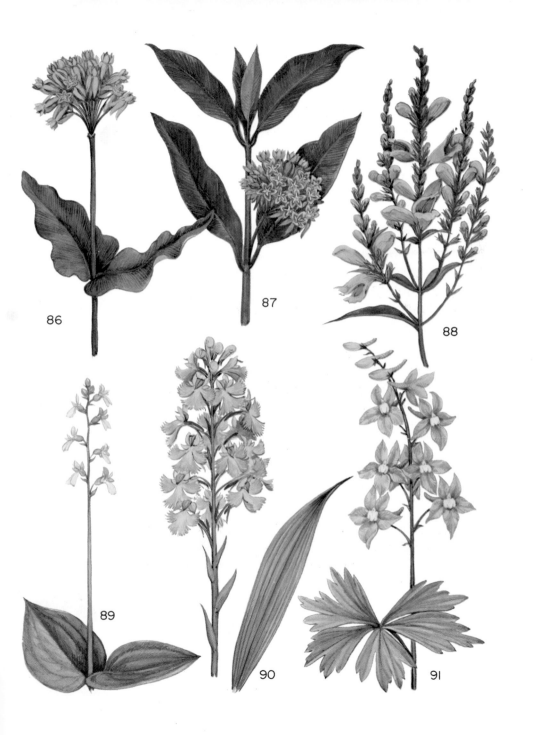

86

87

88

89

90

91

PLATE 16

92. Pickerelweed—*Pontederia cordata*. Violet blue. 1-3 ft. Dense 4-in. spikes of flowers, each marked with yellow-green spot. Triangular leaves a rich dark green. Thrives along the shores of ponds and lakes. A favorite food of the Adirondacks' deer. Blooms in summer. May pick.

93. Spiked Lobelia—*Lobelia spicata*. Pale blue. 1-4 ft. Delicate spires of bloom reach up through deep meadow grass in June. Blooms in sunny dry areas. May pick.

94. Lupine—*Lupinus perennis*. Blue, yellow. 1-2 ft. Grows on Cape Cod near locust groves. Texas Bluebonnets—*Lupinus texensis*. State Flower of Texas. Blooms, summer, in woodland and sunny, sandy soil. Don't pick.

95. Vipers' Bugloss, Blueweed—*Echium vulgare*. Blue. 1-2 ft. Naturalized from Europe where it was believed to relieve a "commotion of the mind." Rough and bristly urn-shaped flowers terminate leafy branches. Summer blooming in sunny meadows. May pick.

96. Asiatic Dayflower—*Commelina communis*. Light blue. 1-3 ft. Naturalized from Asia. Observe fascinating detail of flower structure under a magnifying glass. Blooms in summer almost everywhere. Slightly fragrant. May pick.

97. Blue Curls, Bastard Pennyroyal—*Trichostema dichotomum*. Violet. 6-20 ins. Small "buttonhook" stamens curl outward, hence the name. Blooms summer and fall in warm sunny meadows. May pick.

92

93

94

95

96

97

PLATE 17

98. Bottle Gentian, Closed Gentian—*Gentiana andrewsi.* Ultramarine blue. 1-2 ft. Clusters of bottle-shaped blossoms which stay shut. Blooms summer, fall, in high and low woodlands, along streambanks. Don't pick.

99. Chicory, Succory—*Cichorium intybus.* Violet blue. 1-3 ft. Grows in waste places, seashore areas. Flowers open in morning, close in afternoon. Blooms summer, fall, everywhere, in sunshine. May pick.

100. Great Lobelia—*Lobelia siphilitica.* Light blue-violet. 1-3 ft. Striped blossoms unfold all the way up stalk, opening at bottom first. Blooms summer, fall, in wet pastures. Don't pick.

101. Harebell, Bluebell—*Campanula rotundifolia.* Blue-violet. 6-18 ins. Thrives at sea level and up to 5000 feet, from coast to coast. Famous Bluebells of Scotland. Blooms summer, fall. Acid to neutral soil. May pick.

102. Ironweed—*Vernonia noveboracensis.* Madder purple. 3-7 ft. Purple blooms in bristly flower heads resemble shaggy Bachelor's Buttons. Blooms summer, fall, in moist fields in sun or semishade. May pick.

103. Marsh Rosemary, Sea Lavender—*Limonium carolinianum.* Lavender. 1-2 ft. Naked branches of tiny bloom turn the fringes of beaches lavender. Blooms summer, fall, along sandy shores and in marsh areas. May pick.

98   99   100

101   102   103

PLATE 18

104. New England Aster—*Aster novae-angliae.* Purple-blue. 2-6 ft. Gold-centered flowers in great clusters survive several frosts. Blooms in summer, fall; in sunny meadows, at the fringe of woodlands, along roadsides. May pick.

105. Nightshade—*Solanum dulcamara.* Violet-purple. 2-8 ft. Star-shaped flowers with bright yellow centers. Often called Deadly Nightshade, as the berries are poisonous. Blooms summer, fall, in low woodlands. Don't pick.

106. Purple Coneflower—*Brauneria purpurea.* Deep magenta. 2-3 ft. Two-toothed drooping petals, with a high-tufted, purple cone center. Rough hairy stem. Blossoms summer and fall in sunny meadows. May pick.

107. Rabbit-foot Clover—*Trifolium arvense.* Warm gray-blue. 4-10 ins. Oblong, sweet-scented flower heads. Soft as a kitten's fur. Blooms summer and fall in sunny fields, in poor soil, and in dry rocky fields. May pick.

108. Wild Bergamot—*Monarda fistulosa.* Lavender. 2-3 ft. Coarse plant, shaggy flowers, petals twisted and twirled. Sweet meadow fragrance. Acid to neutral soil. Blooms summer, fall, in sunny fields. May pick.

109. Fringed Gentian—*Gentiana crinita.* Blue. 1-3 ft. Pointed vase-shaped buds unfold into fringed flowers, each with a white throat. Favorite subject of poem and song. Blooms in fall in moist meadows and damp areas, also in dry, semishaded places. Don't pick.

104

105

106

107

108

109

PLATE 19

110. Bellwort—*Uvularia sessilifolia.* Corn yellow. 6-13 ins. Stemless leaves have fine hairs on the underside. Pendulous flowers protect pollen from wind and weather. Blooms, spring, in high and low woodland. Acid soil. Don't pick.

111. Blue Cohosh—*Caulophyllum thalictroides.* Greenish-yellow. 1-3 ft. Purple-blue fold of leaves comes through ground early, and blue fruit follows flower. Blooms in spring in low woodland. Acid to neutral soil. Don't pick.

112. California Poppy—*Eschscholtzia californica.* Yellow-orange. 1-2 ft. State Flower of California. Gray-green lacy foliage. Petals like pressed tissue paper. Blooms in spring, in hot sunny meadows. Don't pick.

113. Dog's-Tooth Violet, Fawn Lily—*Erythronium americanum.* Yellow and brown. 5-10 ins. Dances in the breeze in filtered sunlight along streambanks. Blooms in spring. Acid soil. Don't pick.

114. Lady's-Slipper—*Cypripedium parviflorum.* Deep yellow. 12-18 ins. Fragrant. Brown petals twist above the golden "slipper." Spring blooms in low and high woodlands. Acid to neutral soil. Don't pick.

115. Marsh Marigold—*Caltha palustris.* Golden yellow. 8-15 ins. Grows along the banks of shallow streams. The brilliant flowers are among the first to welcome spring. Acid to neutral soil. Don't pick.

110

111

112

113

114

115

PLATE 20

116. Scotch Broom—*Cytisus scoparius.* Yellow. 2-4 ft. Naturalized from Europe. Make a hearth brush from stiff bushy foliage. Spring blooms in sunny open fields and semi-shaded woodlands. May pick.

117. Dandelion—*Taraxacum officinale.* Yellow. 3-14 ins. If we weren't so indignant about our lawns, we'd appreciate this flower more. It is really beautiful. Enchanting globe-shaped seed clusters. Each seed becomes a small ballerina and dances off to grow elsewhere. Blooms heavily in spring, off and on all summer, everywhere. May pick.

118. Rough-fruited Cinquefoil—*Potentilla recta.* Yellow. 1-2 ft. A coarse tweedy kind of plant originally from Europe. Blooms spring and summer in warm meadows. Don't pick.

119. Sundrop—*Oenothera fruticosa.* Yellow. 1-3 ft. Pure gold blossoms, like captured sunlight. Blooms spring, summer, in sunny meadows. May pick.

120. Bush Honeysuckle—*Diervilla lonicera.* Yellow. 3-4 ft. Break off blossom and suck the base for its honey-sweet nectar. Blooms spring, summer, everywhere in sunlight. May pick.

121. Buttercup—*Ranunculus acris.* Yellow. 2-3 ft. shiny five-petaled flower, slightly hairy plant. Blooms spring and summer everywhere. May pick.

122. Golden Alexanders, Early Meadow Parsnip—*Zizia aurea.* Golden yellow. 2-3 ft. Loose clusters of airy golden flowers. Fine in bouquets. Blooms spring, summer. May pick.

116

117

118

119

120

121

122

PLATE 21

123. False Heather, Woolly Hudsonia—*Hudsonia tomentosa*. Yellow. 5-10 ins. Grows on sandy banks along the shore. Plant and flower both down covered. Blooms spring, summer. May pick.

124. Five-Finger—*Potentilla canadensis*. Yellow. 16-20 in. Runners on ground. Shiny saw-edged leaves. Blooms spring, summer, in sunny meadows. Don't pick.

125. Yellow Pond Lily, Spatterdock—*Nymphaea advena*. Yellow. Flowers float on the surface of lakes, ponds, and meadow bogs, all across the country. Blooms spring and summer. Don't pick.

126. Swamp Buttercup—*Ranunculus septentrionalis*. Deep yellow. 1-2 ft. Shiny petals reflect yellow; hold a flower under your chin and see if you like butter. Blooms spring, summer, in sunny meadows. May pick.

127. Star Grass—*Hypoxis hirsuta*. Yellow. 3-6 ins. Wide-eyed, starry, gold flowers open at the top of a slim stalk. Half-hidden in deep grass. Blooms spring, summer, in sunny pastures. Don't pick.

128. Artemisia—*Artemisia caudata*. Yellow. 2-5 ft. Silvery-gray foliage like coarse velvet lace. Grows along the beaches and salt marshes of Cape Cod. Blooms summer. May pick.

129. Butterfly Weed—*Asclepias tuberosa*. Orange. 1-2 ft. A drop of sweet nectar rests on its petals, so this plant is frequently covered with small brown butterflies and bees. Blooms, summer, in sunny dry meadows. Don't pick.

123

124

125

126

127

128

129

PLATE 22

130. Canada Lily, Yellow Meadow Lily—*Lilium canadense.* Buff yellow. Spotted purple-brown. 2-5 ft. Nodding flowers protect nectar from rain. On a sunny morning myriads of bees move from flower to flower. Blooms, summer, everywhere. Acid soil. Don't pick.

131. Day Lily—*Hemerocallis fulva.* Tawny orange. 2-5 ft. A native of Europe and Asia. Name from the Greek, "beautiful for a day." Blooms summer, in meadows, and at edge of woodland. May pick.

132. Devil's-Paintbrush, Canada Hawkweed—*Hieracium canadense.* Pure yellow. 1-2 ft. Blooms by the acre in sunny June meadows; undulates and flows almost like a river in the breeze. Blooms in summer, everywhere. Don't pick.

133. Downy False Foxglove—*Gerardia flava.* Lemon yellow. 2-4 ft. Foliage velvety. Host to bumblebees and the Peacock butterfly. Summer blooms in meadows and along roadsides. May pick.

134. Evening Primrose—*Oenothera biennis.* Pure yellow. 1-3 ft. Lemon-scented flowers open at dusk. Fertilized after dark by moths. Blooms summertime in sunny meadows. May pick.

135. Loosestrife, Swamp Candle—*Lysimachia terrestris.* Yellow. 1-2 ft. Masses of starry flower-spikes create a gold mist over the meadow. Blooms, summer, in wet pastures. May pick.

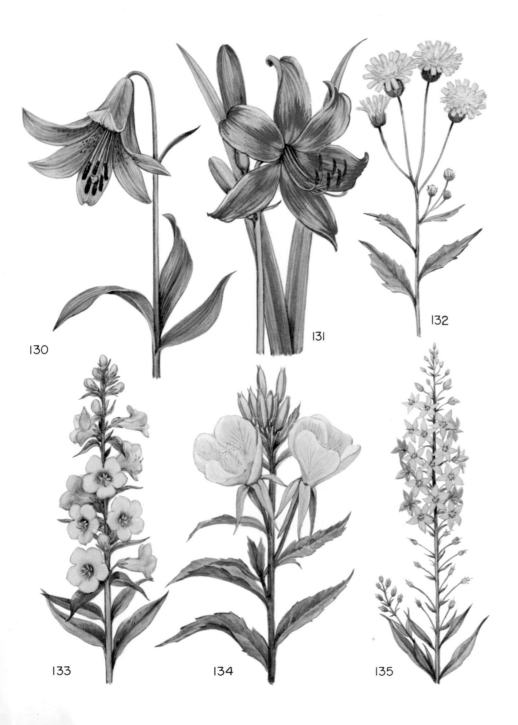

130

131

132

133

134

135

PLATE 23

136. Moneywort, Creeping Charlie—*Lysimachia nummularia.* Yellow. 1-3 ft., trailing stems. Round, creeping, short-stemmed leaves are starred with five-petaled flowers bright as pirate's gold. Blooms summer in wet pastures. May pick.

137. Rattlebox—*Crotalaria sagittalis.* Yellow. 4-12 ins. Seed pods form while flowers are still unfolding. Seeds rattle in boxlike black pods. Blooms, summer, in sunny fields. May pick.

138. Turk's-Cap Lily—*Lilium superbum.* Buff orange, no spots. 3-7 ft. Reflex petals suggest Turkish headdress. The Monarch butterflies depend on it as a source of nectar. Blooms, summer, everywhere. Don't pick.

139. Yellow Mountain Saxifrage—*Leptasea aizoides.* Yellow. 2-7 ins. Grows in northern United States, Europe, Asia, Alps, and Arctic. Thrives on dripping rocks, in hills and mountains. Blooms summer. Don't pick.

140. Black-eyed Susan, Coneflower—*Rudbeckia hirta.* Golden yellow. 2-3 ft. Ripe yellow pollen is carried by bees and butterflies. Blooms summer, fall, in sunny meadows. May pick.

141. Butter-and-Eggs, Toad Flax—*Linaria vulgaris.* Yellow and orange. 1-3 ft. Bee lights on orange lip, flower opens, bee enters, then backs out covered with pollen. Blooms, summer and fall, in sunny meadows. May pick.

142. Clammy ground Cherry—*Physalis heterophylla.* Green-yellow. 1-3 ft. Sticky, hairy stems and heart-shaped leaves. Blooms summer, fall, in low woodlands. May pick.

136

137

138

139

140

141

142

PLATE 24

143 Common Saint-John's-Wort—*Hypericum perforatum.* Golden yellow. 1-2 ft. Five-petaled fragrant blooms have stamens like little gold-tipped pins. Blooms summer, fall, everywhere. May pick.

144. Fever flower, Fern-leaved False Foxglove—*Gerardia pedicularia.* Yellow. 1-3 ft. Fernlike plant blooms summer, fall, almost everywhere. May pick.

145. Goldenrod—*Solidago canadensis.* Golden yellow. 3-7 ft. A plant we gave Europe, now naturalized there. Harbinger of autumn. Thrives in sunny meadows and at fringes of woodland, along stone walls. Acid soil. May pick.

146. Great Mullein—*Verbascum thapsus.* Yellow. 2-6 ft. Fragrant flowers, buds, and seed pods occur simultaneously on tall stalk. Velvety leaves. Blooms, summer, in dry sunny meadows or along roadsides. May pick.

147. Hop Clover—*Trifolium agrarium.* Yellow. 6-15 ins. Withered florets droop, turn brown, and resemble dried hops. Blooms summer, fall, in sunny meadows. May pick.

148. Jewelweed, Touch-me-not—*Impatiens biflora.* Golden yellow. 2-5 ft. A blossom with red-brown freckles. Hummingbirds love it. Touch pods and they snap open. Blooms summer, fall, in woodlands and along the roadsides. May pick.

143

144

145

146

147

148

PLATE 25

149. Lance-leaved Goldenrod—*Solidago graminifolia.* Golden yellow. 2-4 ft. Flat clusters of fragrant flowers, slim downy leaves. Blooms summer, fall. Grows everywhere. Acid soil. May pick.

150. Partridge Pea—*Cassia chamaecrista.* Yellow. 1-2 ft. Hairy pods follow bloom. Leaves fold when touched, but will open again. Blooms summer and fall in sunny meadows. Don't pick.

151. Poor-Robin's-Plantain, Rattlesnake Weed—*Hieracium venosum.* Golden yellow. 12-20 ins. Leaves attractively bordered, veined, and ribbed with dull magenta. Blooms summer, fall, in high dry woodlands. May pick.

152. Seaside Goldenrod—*Solidago sempervirens.* Golden yellow. 2-4 ft. Flower heads brilliant against a backdrop of blue water. Leaves smooth. Blooms summer, fall, in sunny sandy areas. May pick.

153. Sunflower—*Helianthus annuus.* Yellow. 2-10 ft. Native to the West. Flowers yield honey and dye; stalks are used for textile fiber. Blooms summer and fall, in sunny, dry places. May pick.

154. Giant Sunflower—*Helianthus giganteus.* Yellow. 3-12 ft. Grows all through the East along roadsides and in damp meadows. Blooms summer, fall. May pick.

155. Fall Dandelion—*Leontodon autumnalis.* Golden yellow. 7-15 ins. Many-lobed, narrow leaves. Fringed flower catches and holds autumn sunlight. Blooms, fall, in sunny meadows. May pick.

149

150

151

152

153

154

155

PINK, PURPLE-RED, AND RED

PLATE 26

156. Columbine—*Aquilegia canadensis.* Scarlet and yellow. 1-2 ft. Stand quietly and watch ruby-throated hummingbirds come to sip. Blooms in spring in low and high woodlands, sometimes in sunny meadows. Acid to neutral soil. Don't pick.
Long-spurred Blue Columbine—*Aquilegia caerulea.* State Flower of Colorado. Don't pick.

157. Moccasin Flower—*Cypripedium acaule.* Crimson pink. 8-12 ins. Pink slipper is deeply veined, has three brown petals. Blooms in spring, low and high woodlands, beneath oak and pine. Acid soil. Don't pick.

158. Showy Orchis—*Orchis spectabilis.* Magenta and white. 5-10 ins. Found in hemlock groves. Flower stalk emerges between a pair of shiny green leaves. Spring blooming in low woodland. Moderately acid soil. Don't pick.

159. Spring Beauty—*Claytonia virginica.* Pale pink or white. 6-12 ins. From the midst of ribbon-like leaves perky flowers emerge. Each is five-petalled, with deeper veins and gold stamens. Bloom spring, low woodlands. Moderately acid soil. Don't pick.

160. Trailing Arbutus, Mayflower—*Epigaea repens.* Pink and white. 6-12 ins. Grows on evergreen hillsides and rock ledges. Waxy flowers fragrant and beautiful. Spring blooms. Acid soil. Don't pick.

161. Wake-Robin, Birthroot—*Trillium erectum.* Maroon. 7-15 inches. Nodding blossoms appear above three deep-green leaves. Blooms in spring, high and low woodlands, along stone walls. Acid soil. Don't pick.

156

157

158

159

160

161

PLATE 27

162. Wild Pink—*Silene caroliniana.* Scarlet. 10 ins. Starry blooms blanket the mountainsides of North Carolina. Blooms spring, at woodland fringes. May pick.

163. Moss Pink—*Phlox subulata.* Crimson. 2-5 ins. Grows like thick green moss, starred with crimson flowers. Blooms spring, summer, in sunny fields, and on banks. Don't pick.

164. Atamasco Lily—*Zephyranthes atamasco.* Pink or white, tinged with magenta. 6-15 ins. Named for the West Wind, *Zephyros.* Slender stalks, ribbon-like leaves. Blooms spring, summer; wet pastures, woodlands. Don't pick.

165. Beach Pea—*Lathyrus maritimus.* Magenta. 1-2 ft. Thrives in pure sand on Cape Cod. Lovely blue-green foliage. Blooms spring, summer. Don't pick.

166. Coral Honeysuckle—*Lonicera sempervirens.* Coral pink. 8-15 ft., climbing. Tubular clusters of flowers like bunches of small firecrackers. Blooms spring, summer, in sunny fields and woodland fringes. May pick.

167. Dragon's-Mouth, Swamp Pink—*Arethusa bulbosa.* Light magenta, crimson. 5-10 ins. A fragrant wild orchid named for the stream-nymph, Arethusa. Blooms spring, summer, in low woodlands. Don't pick.

168. Indian Paintbrush—*Castilleja coccinea.* Salmon, red, purple. 1-2 ft. State Flower of Wyoming. Striking amid the gray sagebrush. Blooms spring, summer, on hot dry prairies and mesas. May pick.

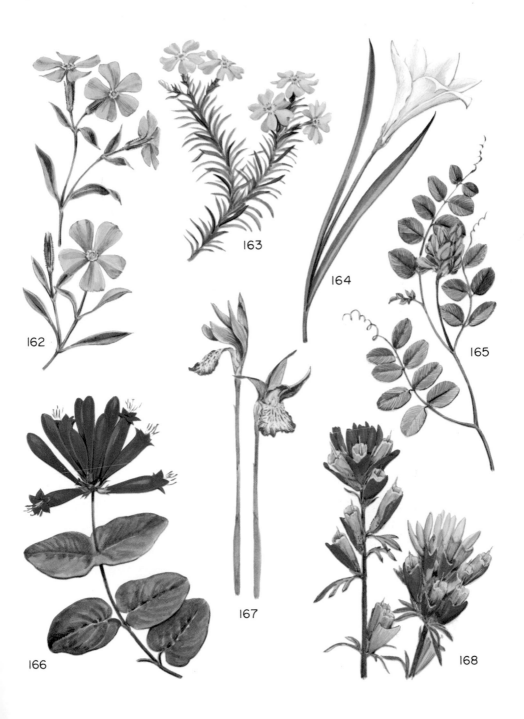

162

163

164

165

166

167

168

PLATE 28

169. Pitcher Plant, Sidesaddle Flower—*Sarracenia purpurea.* Dull dark red. 4-10 ins. The reddish-green pitchers have bristles that trap insects. Blooms spring, summer, in low woodlands and boggy areas. Don't pick.

170. Wood Betony, Lousewort—*Pedicularis canadensis.* Red and yellow. 6-10 ins. Bunched blossoms on a cushion of reddish, feathery leaves. Blooms spring and summer in sunny meadows. Acid to neutral soil. May pick.

171. Bouncing Bet, Soapwort—*Saponaria officinalis.* Magenta, pink, and white. 1-2 ft. Petal edges; scalloped fragrance spicy. Blooms summer in sunny meadows and along roadsides. May pick.

172. Fireweed, Spiked Willow-Herb—*Epilobium angustifolium.* Magenta. 4-7 ft. Flowers spring up in burned-over areas. On each stalk at one time are bud, flower, and seed pod. Blooms in summer everywhere. Acid to neutral soil. May pick.

173. Flaming Sword, Ocotillo—*Fouquieria splendens.* Red. 6-15 ft. Grows in Arizona, California, New Mexico. In spring each forbidding thorny stalk is covered with smooth, friendly, apple-like leaves. After the rains, flower clusters appear among the spines. Blooms in summer in desert areas. Don't pick.

174. Maiden Pink—*Dianthus deltoides.* Crimson-pink. 6-12 ins. Flowers in drifts in old Cape Cod cemeteries. Blooms summer in sunny fields. May pick.

169

170

171

172

173

174

PLATE 29

175. Marsh Pink—*Sabatia dodecandra.* Crimson. 1-2 ft. Oblong leaf, deep pink flower, yellow center. Grows in sunny wet spots, summer-blooming. May pick.

176. Meadowsweet, Quaker-Lady—*Spiraea latifolia.* Flesh pink. 2-4 ft. Pyramidal flower spike with feathery blooms. Sweetly fragrant. Comes in summer. Grows in meadows and along roadsides. May pick.

177. Sheep Laurel, Lambskill—*Kalmia angustifolia.* Crimson pink. 3-5 ft. New leaves above bloom in center of stem. Flowers, summer, in sunny wet pastures. Don't pick.

178. Spiked Loosestrife—*Lythrum salicaria.* Magenta. 2-3 ft. Grows in sunny, low areas near water. Thrives along the Housatonic River in Connecticut. Blooms summer. May pick.

179. Swamp Rose—*Rosa carolina.* Pink. 2-7 ft. Wonderfully fragrant, especially after rain. Old recipe for sandwich filling: petals and butter mixture stored in covered jar for two days. Summer-blooming in sunny meadows, wet or dry. May pick.

180. Twinflower, Deer Vine—*Linnaea borealis.* Crimson pink. 2-5 ft. A trailing vine with reddish woody stems and pairs of bell-shaped flowers. Blooms summer in meadows and along roadsides. Acid soil. May pick.

181. Western Bleeding Heart—*Dicentra formosa.* Pink and rosy purple. 2 ft. Heart-shaped blossoms on arching stalk; feathery gray-green foliage. Found in Yosemite Valley, Oregon, and Washington. Blooms summer, in acid soil. May pick.

175

176

177

178

179

180

181

PLATE 30

182. Wood Lily—*Lilium philadelphicum.* Orange-scarlet, spotted purple-brown. 1-3 ft. Unlike many Lilies: flower cup opens upward and petals stand apart. Blooms, summer, in sunny meadow, or at edge of woodland. Acid soil. Don't pick.

183. Cardinal Flower, Red Lobelia—*Lobelia cardinalis.* Deep red. 2-4 ft. Showy flower spikes pollinated by hummingbirds. Blooms summer, fall, along streams and edge of woodland. Don't pick.

184. Coast Jointweed—*Polygonella articulata.* Dusty pink. 4-12 ins. Feathery flowers and foliage. Coastal areas Maine to Florida. Blooms tint the beach pink in summer and fall. May pick.

185. Common Thistle—*Cirsium lanceolatum.* Magenta. 2-4 ft. Bristly, thorny, unfriendly—but beautiful. Each charming seed attached to a small parachute of down. Blooms summer and fall everywhere. May pick.

186. Deptford Pink—*Dianthus armeria.* Crimson pink. 6-18 ins. An herbal brew of pinks cheers the heart and eliminates melancholy. Blooms summer, fall, in sunny meadows. Do pick.

187. Hempweed Vine, Boneset—*Mikania scandens.* Flesh pink. 5-15 ft., climbing. Flowers grow in clusters on short stalks and emerge where leaf stem joins vine. Blooms summer, fall, in low woodlands and sunny pastures. Don't pick.

182

183

184

185

186

187

PLATE 31

188. Joe-Pye Weed—*Eupatorium purpureum*. Dusty magenta. 3-12 ft. Flowers composed of soft bristles; coarse leaf and stem. Announces fall. Flourishes in low woodlands and along streams. May pick.

189. Lady's-Thumb, Heartweed—*Polygonum persicaria*. Crimson pink. 1-2 ft. Common in waste places. Dusty pink in autumn sunlight. Blooms summer through late fall. May pick.

190. Milkwort—*Polygala sanguinea*. Magenta-pink. 6-12 ins. Flowers suggest a smaller version of clover. Blooms summer, fall, in meadows and wet pastures. May pick.

191. Oswego Tea, American Bee Balm—*Monarda didyma*. Scarlet red. 2 ft. Host to hummingbirds; stand quietly and watch as they visit. Blooms summer, fall, along streambanks and in woodlands. Acid soil. May pick.

192. Pinesap, Beechdrops—*Monotropa hypopitys*. Tawny-reddish. 4-12 ins. Thrives under oaks and pine. Urn-shaped flowers with a vague fragrance. Acid soil. Don't pick.

193. Ragged Robin, Cuckoo Flower—*Lychnis flos-cuculi*. Pink or crimson. 1-2 ft. Ragged, shredded flower petals. Found in old European gardens. Blooms summer, fall, in sunny damp areas. May pick.

194. Rugosa Rose—*Rosa rugosa*. Pink, white. 2-4 ft. Grows in pure sand along the shore. Make hips into jam or a healthy vitamin-C drink. Fragrant blooms summer and fall in sunny, open areas. Do pick.

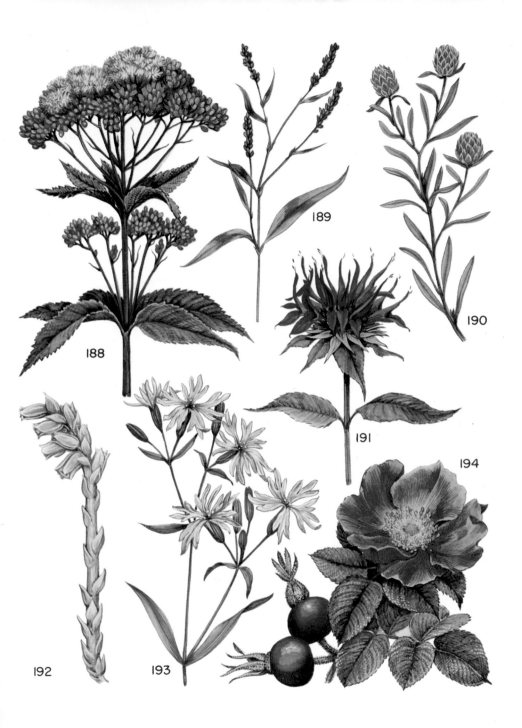

188

189

190

191

192

193

194

PLATE 32

195. Sand Verbena—*Abronia villosa.* Lilac-pink, creeping. Light blue-green leaves straggle over the desert sands of Utah, Arizona, and California. Very fragrant blooms come in summer, fall. Do pick.

196. Slender Gerardia—*Gerardia tenuifolia.* Magenta. 10-20 ins. Flowers like little flaring trumpets; leaves like short, sharp darning needles. Named for the famous botanist, John Gerarde. Blooms summer, fall, in sunny meadows. Do pick.

197. Small-leaved Burdock—*Arctium minus.* Magenta. 4-8 ft. Coarse foliage, leaves woolly beneath. Burrs cling and go where you go to take up a new life far from home-base. Blooms summer, fall, in sunny meadows and gravelly waste areas. Don't pick.

198. Steeplebush, Hardhack—*Spiraea tomentosa.* Deep pink. 2-4 ft. Steeple-like flower spike with a succession of blooms, opening from the top down. Woolly stems. Olive green leaves, white and woolly underneath. Blooms summer, fall, in damp areas with sun or semi-shade. Do pick.

199. Swamp Rose Mallow—*Hibiscus moscheutos.* Pale pink, white. 4-6 ft. Blooms summer, fall, in sunny bogs. Don't pick.

200. Woodsage, American Germander—*Teucrium canadense.* Pale purple, magenta. 1-2 ft. Downy leaves, especially hairy on underside. Flowers arranged in circles around the stalk. Broad lower lip makes a fine landing-place for bees. Blooms in summer, fall, in low woodlands and sunny bogs. May pick.

195

196

197

198

199

200

Part II

WILD FLOWERS TO GROW

A wild garden is not a garden that has run wild, reminding us of man's neglect; it is a poetic suggestion of the beauty of Nature untouched by man.

—WILHELM MILLER

3. Nature Holds the Key

Isn't every flower wild somewhere? Lupines run rampant in Texas, Primroses in England, Orchids in Guatemala, Crocuses and Daffodils in Switzerland, to name just a few. If a definition is needed, perhaps a wild flower may be defined as any flower native to a region. No matter how you define wild flowers, once you begin to know them, you want to grow them, and growing them becomes a fascinating pastime.

To our joy after moving to Connecticut, we found we lived in the midst of more than a hundred wild flower varieties. That first season was a constant miracle of discovery. I'll never forget one July day when I saw my first Wood Lily—a flash of flaming copper-red in the meadow. I looked it up in my reference books, and by the time its neighbors bloomed the next week they seemed like old friends.

So many people think of wild flowers as being purely beauties of spring. Actually, as many bloom in August and September as in May. The spring wild flowers, Hepatica, Bloodroot, Dutchman's-Breeches, are the more delicate, the more subtle in their beauty—like spring itself. Midsummer brings brilliant Black-eyed Susans, vivid Butterfly Weed, and stately Yucca, with a sense of drama that is continued by smoky-blue fall Asters, magenta Joe-Pye Weed, and glowing Sunflowers.

Sights and Sensations

The better we came to know the wild flowers on our land, the more we wanted to keep all of them, add to those already thriving, and introduce new varieties. We were stirred by the Blue and Fringed Gentians on the hillside beyond our land. Would some grow for us? We wanted to have some Dutchman's-Breeches like those flourishing on the damp, stony banks in our woods. Lavender Bee Balm, Columbine, Trillium—all challenged us.

When it came to landscaping our new place, we decided to skip the formality of borders, beds, and sweeps of lawn and go along with nature instead, helping the wild flowers take over. We have never regretted our decision. The naturalized wildings save us lots of work. As natives, they don't need our attention for watering, spraying, lifting, dividing, mowing, or cultivating. And the weeds that do occasionally crowd in are easy to ignore because a few weeds, after all, belong in a natural setting. Besides, what is a weed? Usually it is just a misplaced wild flower. Working with nature in nature's way has been easier and, to us, more satisfying than laboring to establish a new order of our own making.

The secret of success in growing wild flowers is to grow the right plant in the right place. A wild flower thrives where soil, sun, and water exactly suit its needs. In proper season, it beguiles you with bloom, and then blends into the background to finish its cycle of growth, while another plant flowers.

Strength and Charm

Each year the annuals reseed themselves, while the perennials resprout from hardy roots—all flourishing without the helping hand of man. Beyond their obvious beauty, wild flowers have an exuberant quality of vigor and great good health, the same appealing quality you see in a frisky colt or a robust child at play. This is guaranteed in wild flowers.

On our place we have added more than a dozen different kinds of wild flowers to the hundred-plus already established there. Our method is simplicity itself. We let the flowers show us where they like to grow. We learn all we can about them in the wild and try to establish only those for which we can provide similar conditions at home.

First, you learn the special character of your own land and the variations in soil, in water run-off, in sun, and shade.

And then comes the great adventure of searching out wild flowers and observing why they grow where they do. From now on you will look at the meadows and woods, the roads and the byways from a new point of view.

POINTS TO NOTE

Your first field trip is mainly for information. Whenever you find a flower that appeals to you, sketch or photograph it, study it awhile, and then record the following specific points:

Location. There are five general classifications: (1) high, dry woodland; (2) low woodland or brookside; (3) dry pasture or meadow, or roadside; (4) wet pasture or meadow, ditch, or bog; (5) fringe of woodland.

Soil. Note the kind of soil the plant you want grows in. Pick up a handful. Feel it. Is it rocky, clayish, loamy, full of leaf mold, or what? The closer you can approximate this soil at home, the better it will be for the plant.

Slope of Land. Are the flowers growing on a north, south, east, or west slope? (A compass will be helpful here.) This determines to a degree how much sun and soil warmth the plant will get during the day. Plants growing wild on an open south slope receive a lot of sun and they obviously will need the same amount in your garden. Flowers on the north slope get less. The slope also tells you a lot about drainage. Plants found on a steep hillside usually will not thrive in a boggy site; those in a gully or on flat land are not so particular about drainage. And this, of course, is also related to soil structure.

Sun and Shade. Are the plants of your choice growing in full sun, full shade, or half shade? Are they shaded in the morning or afternoon? As you become more observant you will find variations in shade you may never have noticed before. There is a difference in the dense shade of low bushes, the light shade of taller ones, and the open shade of high trees. Also, evergreens cast a dense year-round shade, while deciduous shade is variable. These conditions all affect growth.

Special Conditions. Some flowers are at their best growing over rocks, around the roots of trees, on the sunny side of a fallen log, or in the lee of a stump or stone wall. When you find flowers flourishing in a special place, that's just the location to give them in their new home. Record this in your notebook.

The Intangibles. Try to sense the feeling—the atmosphere—of the location. This will sharpen your sensibilities and awareness of such things as the hush in pine woods where Indian Pipes send up waxy white flowers, or the feeling of riotous gaiety in a meadow of flaming golden Hawkweed.

As you select flowers to naturalize, keep in mind that it is always easier to go along with what is. It is better to find the plant to suit the soil you have than to take on the project of altering the conditions to suit the plant you want. Follow the ancient Chinese proverb, "Hurry slowly and you soon arrive."

We began by buying and bringing to our acres just a few varieties of such favorites as Dutchman's-Breeches, American Bee Balm, and Bouncing Bet. As these became established, we gradually expanded the plantings. In a project like this, you forget about dozens and think in terms of hundreds and even thousands of plants. You may not personally set out hundreds, but this will be your eventual goal. If your selections have been right for your conditions, the plants will increase of their own accord.

BUY, GROW, COLLECT

You can buy wild flowers, you can raise them from seed, you can collect them. Collecting them from woods, roadsides, fields, and streambanks is one of our favorite pastimes.

Early spring is a good time to move many wild flowers,

as they are then easy to find and to recognize. By summer, they will be buried under lush growth. We have successfully moved Hepaticas, Columbine, Dutchman's-Breeches, Foamflower, and Bloodroot when they were just about to bloom. Summer-flowering wildlings, such as Beardtongue, Daisies, Black-eyed Susans, Goldenrod, and others, will do well if taken when the plants are 6 to 10 inches high, which is in early June here.

Fall is also a good time to collect. Mark in spring with rocks and stakes what you plan to dig in fall. Summer moving isn't impossible, but it is difficult unless you have had a very rainy week. If you are moving a tall plant that has finished flowering, cut the tops back to facilitate handling.

LAW OF THE LAND

Keep in mind that all land belongs to someone and that there are laws concerning the gathering of wild flowers. Check first the conservation list in Chapter 16, and be sure to get permission from the owners before you take any plants or even enter private grounds.

It is fortunate for both you and the plants if you find a place where there is a building or highway under construction. What a gold mine such an area yields. Here you can always get permission to help yourself to wildlings that would otherwise be destroyed. You will feel like a good Samaritan as you save basketsful from destruction. And, of course, here you are not only permitted but encouraged to dig *any* and *all* plants even those on your state conservation list. Take small trees, too, before they are bulldozed. Young, 2- to 3-foot Dogwoods and Hemlocks are especially easy to dig and transplant.

Equipment for Gathering

To bring plants from the wild, you will need flats or baskets, burlap bags, newspapers, shovel, pruning shears, trowel, large pieces of cellophane, plastic bags, and a jug of water or a pail for carrying water. In digging, disturb roots as little as possible. Take as much surrounding earth as practicable with each plant.

Suppose, to be specific, that it is May when you are going to dig up a 6-inch-high Black-eyed Susan. First, clear away leaves, grasses, and litter that obstruct the process. Make a circular cut, say 10 inches in diameter and 8 inches deep, around the plant. Adjust the diameter of the cut to the size of the plant and its depth to the length of its roots. Perhaps in one cut a foot in diameter you'll get three or four plants. In digging you may sever some of the outside roots with your sharp shovel, and to dig up a bigger plant you may have to cut one or two larger

86

roots with the pruning shears. No harm will be done. With your spade or shovel, gently lift out the root ball, first having loosened it on one side and then on the other. Disturb soil around the roots as little as possible. Wrap the clump in newspapers or a plastic sheet to hold soil together, or slip it into a plastic bag.

The wildling will be more at home in your garden with some extra earth from where it grew. If you are taking ten Black-eyed Susans, a bushelbasket of soil from the same meadow will make them thoroughly at home.

Suppose you are transplanting a creeper like Partridge-berry. (And you can only dig this in the path of a bull-dozer as it is on the protected list in most states.) Instead of taking a root ball, ease the long root stems out of the ground, coil them up, and put the plant in a plastic bag with a couple of handfuls of wet sphagnum moss.

In digging small trees, you'll be surprised at the length of the taproot in many cases, even with very young seed-lings. Get as much of this root as you can. Keep tree seedlings wrapped in wet sphagnum and newspapers or plastic for the trip home. Dig only as much as you can plant the same day, for wildlings should not remain over-night out of the earth.

When you get home, set everything in the shade.

Before you plant, check again the selected locations to

make sure they are similar to the ones in which you found the plants.

NATURALIZING AND PLANTING

Naturalizing to me means growing wild plants in casual sweeps. One plant here and there is lost, whereas a massed grouping of the same variety is effective. Set plants out, not only in similar soil and location, but also as close to each other as you found them.

Clear away surrounding growth in an area somewhat larger than that the plants will occupy to give them the elbow room they need to start. When you are ready to set out the first one, dig an oversize hole. By way of example, for our Black-eyed Susan, if there are three or four in a clump and they seem young, leave them together. If they appear to be mature, gently separate tangled roots and stand the plants a foot apart. Take some of the extra meadow soil which you have brought back and place it in the too-large hole under and around each new plant. See that the crown is at the depth at which it grew. Never bury deep nor set high. (For example, you may find a Pink Lady's-Slipper with the growing tip only one inch below the soil's surface.) Now, put in additional soil with your trowel, firm around the plant. Be sure there are no air pockets among the roots. Water thoroughly, toss some

88

grass or other mulch over the ground to hold in the moisture, and the plant will probably never know it has been moved.

The Partridgeberry may be cut into a number of 6- to 10-inch lengths, provided each piece carries a cluster of roots. Put some of its "own" soil under it. Press the soil firmly over the stems, leaving only the small round leaves above the ground. Cover the surrounding area with leaves and other litter, and water well. Water newly-set wild flowers and trees every day until there is a heavy rain. In due time, once they are established, you can leave them in the care of Mother Nature.

One good method of introducing wild flowers to your garden is to bring from the wild three or four of one variety new to your land, and let these be guinea pigs in your chosen site. Observe results for a season. If these plants thrive, acquire more. If not, choose another location or another plant.

There are advantages to buying certain wild flowers. Some you want may not be found in your vicinity or they may be on your state conservation list. In that case, turn to some of the fine wild flower nurseries. These are a boon if you live in a settled community far from woodlands and meadows. In my lists and picture captions, I have indicated the conditions each variety requires for successful growing. This will help you with culture if you cannot actually see plants growing. Try to select those you think you can please.

However, if there is a nursery anywhere near, and if you possibly can, do go in person. Make an appointment and say you want some advice so that the grower will save time for you and be prepared to help. Go early in the morning, discuss your land, situation, and conditions. Take notes on the growing needs of each plant. Buy what you want and get extra soil with each variety. Bring your new plants and extra earth home and *set them out the same day.*

While I have given many specifics on transplanting, wild flower gardening is not merely a matter of fact and rule; it also involves imagination, initiative, and creativity. Mingle all I have said with your own hunches, observation, and intuition. You never know till you try how any wild flower project will come out. But if you let nature and your own feelings for plants be your teacher —if you listen and learn well—you will surely succeed.

4. Seeds, Cuttings, Divisions

Suppose you want hundreds or even thousands of plants —as you probably will once you begin to know wild flowers. Collecting or buying great numbers of plants and then planting each one of them can be a tremendous undertaking. An excellent way to acquire wild flowers in quantity is to propagate your own. Three good methods are: by seeds, by cuttings, by division of roots, bulbs, or corms.

Although propagating by cuttings and division have their purposes and satisfactions, still, sowing seed is usually our choice. Partly because seeds themselves are so completely fascinating.

Milkweed seeds burst out of their pods like opening night at the ballet. Each small brown wafer is attached to a downy parachute that glistens in the sunlight as it is borne off on the breeze to a new home. Jewelweed pods, crisp and brown, at the slightest touch of man or beast spring open to fling their treasured contents far and wide. Angel's-Trumpet seeds ripen in prickle-covered pods. Pink Lady's-Slipper seed is dry brown dust, and yet what beauty emerges! Part of the charm of Violet seeds is how neatly they are tucked in their pods. The ordered arrangement in all seed pods is a particular kind of beauty, and one not to miss as you gather them.

In addition to its physical charms, a seed is a miracle. Here in each little pinhead or speck of dust that lies in your palm is life and beauty, rare and stirring. In a handful lies a potential woodland of beautiful flowers, or maybe a meadow of blazing color and fragrance. In each seed, sealed and ready for use as needed, is enough nourishment to see this new life and its offspring on their way. A seed is a link with yesterday—a step into tomorrow.

PROPAGATE BY SEEDS

Raising plants from seed is delightful. If your favorite wild flower is on the forbidden list, you can still take a handful of seeds from it and end up with not one but a great number of plants! Wild flower seeds germinate most successfully if sown in soil taken from their habitat. You can probably get permission to dig enough soil to fill a flat, but be careful not to disturb nearby plants while digging.

The perfect time for gathering wild flower seeds is right after they form. This will be late spring and the beginning of summer for the early bloomers, fall for summer varieties, and late fall for the last flowers of the year. In other words, from June through October some wild flower is always ripening and forming seed. In your car's glove compartment, keep several envelopes with gummed labels, and one or two large clasp envelopes. Thus, whenever you take an excursion to woods, meadows, or even just a drive over back roads, you will be prepared if you spot something worth bringing home.

Time to Gather

Gather pods wherever they are ripening. Shake the seeds into an envelope. Seal and label immediately. Make a note also of where the flower grows, and further pertinent details. Label with equal care your baskets of soil, especially if you have gathered seed from more than one variety of plant, so you can make the proper connections at home.

If the seeds are not yet ripe, place the pods in the large clasp envelope. At home, spread the pods out in sun until they are crisp and you can shake out the seeds. Be careful where you lay them as they are a delicacy for birds.

You can keep seeds over until the next spring if you store them in a cold place. Sometimes we keep them in our unheated garage, and sow the following May. But, if you possibly can, it is *much* better to plant them right

93

after they are gathered. As I have said, you are most sure of success if you sow them in soil taken from their native site. Of course, you may have an area with comparable soil on your place, but if not, and if you have been unable to collect any native earth, you can prepare your own seeding soil. A good mixture is: equal parts of leaf mold, peat moss, garden loam, and sand.

OPEN OR COVERED PLANTINGS

Seeds may be planted in 3-inch-deep flats or in pots in a coldframe, or greenhouse, or in open ground. The coldframe may be semishaded by trees, buildings, or by lathes. Seeds germinate best in the same degree of sun or shade in which the parent plants grew. Semishade is safe for most varieties.

On our place we have two seed beds in open ground. Each is about 8 by 10 feet. One is in dappled shade, along a stone wall, the other is in a corner of the vegetable garden where it receives a half day of sun. Sowing seeds in open ground is much less demanding, but more perilous too, for birds, mice, and other small creatures eat them. But because open-ground sowing is so much easier, we prefer it. We lose some seeds this way, but come out fairly well in the end.

To create a good seed bed, dig down a spade's depth

and turn over the soil. Remove roots and rocks. If possible, replace the top 2 to 3 inches with soil you have collected. Sift and spread the native earth an inch deep where the seeds are to go. Keep all the little twigs and old leaves that you have sifted out and scatter this litter around the seedlings as they grow. This organic matter releases beneficial elements on which seedlings thrive.

Tiny seeds may be scattered on top of the soil with a dusting of fine soil over them. Larger seeds are planted a half- to a quarter-inch deep. Seeds of some species sprout readily, and many small seedlings appear almost immediately. When these are an inch high they can be separated carefully to stand 3 to 4 inches apart. When they have four true leaves and are 5 to 6 inches tall, move them to their permanent abode. Plants from seed sown in early summer may be ready for their final move the next spring; others, a year later.

FAST OR SLOW

Germination time varies greatly with each species. Fringed Gentian and Daisy Fleabane sprout almost immediately, but many others need a winter of frost and snow before they emerge from their hard coatings. Certain varieties like Columbine or Lady's-Slipper may take two years to germinate. The United State Department of

95

Agriculture experimented with seeds of Wild Morning Glory which, after having been buried for thirty years, sprouted in two days—just to show how long some can wait. Seeds of Lotus, unearthed after an estimated four hundred years in a bog, sprouted and grew into hardy plants. So you never know.

After you sow the seeds, label each section or row in the beds with the name of the species. And, since labels have a way of disappearing, you might make a diagram of how things are arranged as well. Between the two you will know what is what.

EASY METHOD

There is another method of sowing seed that is chancy, but rather fun, and certainly so simple it is worth a trial somewhere on your place. Choose an area where you would like wild flowers, a space that has at present only light vegetation. It is helpful, but not essential, to remove some of the vegetation and loosen the soil in places. Check soil and other conditions in the area and decide which wild flowers (not on a conservation list) you think will thrive there. When your choice has been made, elsewhere, trim off a basketful of plant tops, including seed pods, and toss them over the ground where you'd like them to become naturalized; and await results. If you have been perceptive in matching soil and conditions, the plants may well grow and multiply there.

The State Highway Department of Texas often uses this system. It mows an area where seed is ripening and spreads plant tops along nearby roadsides where other vegetation is thin.

FOR SUCCESS

There are a few general rules for seed-sowing success. Keep seedlings free from weeds; water them in a drought. After the first few frosts, provide a winter leaf cover held down with branches. Use, if possible, the same kind of leaves that grew near that particular plant in its habitat.

The spring after seeds have been sown, some species will be ready for permanent locations. Clear a little space for them in a chosen spot; remove grass roots and surrounding growth. For best effect, plant the way the wildlings grew naturally. As with any young plants, when first set out, they need freedom from competing growth, so for the first two years keep out neighboring plants that tend to crowd them.

PROPAGATE BY CUTTINGS

A cutting is a piece of stem or root that can be encouraged to form its own roots so it can grow into a new plant. Cuttings root best in a coldframe (a simple wooden box with a glass top). The cuttings are set into a moist, porous rooting medium in the coldframe. First bore a few holes in the bottom of the box—but only a few. You don't want water to stand in the box, but neither do you want it to run off too quickly. Sink the box part way into the ground where there is good light but no direct sun. Along the north side of the house can be ideal, or under the shade of high trees. Shade conserves moisture, while exposure to sun dries out the plants too rapidly. The glass covering keeps the degree of humidity high within, where cuttings need it for new root growth.

A good rooting medium consists of equal parts peat moss, well-decayed compost, and sand.

Before you take cuttings to propagate a desirable plant, make sure it is vigorous and free from disease or insects. Each cutting should be 4 to 6 inches long. Make the cuts sharp and clean and just below a leaf bud or joint. Strip off all leaves near the base. Since most plants have the ability to send out roots from a wound in the stem, make a slight cut near the base of the stalk before you set it into the rooting medium. If you wish, you may dip the cut end into a root-inducing hormone preparation (*Rootone, Hormodin*, etc.) and then insert each stem in the rooting mixture to a third of its length. (There are two

schools of thought on the value of root-inducing hor-
mones. We have had success with and without them.)

When you have put in the desired number of sturdy
little cuttings, each one a few inches from the next in
rows, water them and cover with glass. The cuttings must
never dry out. A weekly watering will usually be ade-
quate. When roots have formed, move the new plants into
pots of soil or into the garden.

PROPAGATE BY DIVISIONS

This is an excellent method to use with many wild
flowers. It permits you to multiply economically the plants
you already have. Also, when you buy plants, try to choose
large ones and, if possible, divide them before setting
them out. Thus one large clustered plant may become
many individuals. It couldn't be simpler.

An ideal time to do this is early spring when plants
are up high enough to be recognized, but not in flower.
Choose, for example, a Violet. Lift it from the ground,
loosen the soil about the roots. Gently work the roots
apart, or cut them apart if necessary. Immediately put
each small new Violet in a hole of its own in the garden.
In about two years it will have grown to the size of its
parent—or near it. And how rewarding this is.

We have on our land a little of everything: a brook,

wet woods, a sunny bog, dry woods, dry meadow, rock walls. Hence we have many different kinds of wild flowers. But whether you have all these sites or only one, or whether you are going to create a woodland garden from scratch, there are still any number of wild flowers that you can propagate.

PLANTS TO PROPAGATE BY SEED

White, Variable and Off-White, Green Tints

American Lotus—*Nelumbo lutea*
Bloodroot—*Sanguinaria canadensis*
Bunchberry—*Cornus canadensis*
Clematis—*Clematis virginiana*
Daisy Fleabane—*Erigeron ramosus*
Datura—*Datura stramonium*
False Solomon's-Seal—*Smilacina racemosa*
Large Flowering Trillium—*Trillium grandiflorum*
May Apple—*Podophyllum peltatum*
Solomon's-Seal—*Polygonatum biflorum*

Clear Blue, Lavender, and Purple

Common Milkweed—*Asclepias syriaca*
Fringed Gentian—*Gentiana crinita*
Hepatica—*Hepatica triloba*
Lupine—*Lupinus perennis*
Purple Coneflower—*Brauneria purpurea*
Wild Geranium—*Geranium maculatum*

Yellow, Orange-Yellow, and Orange

Black-eyed Susan—*Rudbeckia hirta*
Butterfly Weed—*Asclepias tuberosa*

SEEDS, CUTTINGS, DIVISIONS

Canada Lily—*Lilum canadense*

Day Lily—*Hemerocallis fulva*

Dog's-Tooth Violet—*Erythronium americanum*

Jewelweed—*Impatiens biflora*

Star Grass—*Hypoxis hirsuta*

Sunflower—*Helianthus giganteus*

Pink, Purple-Red, and Red

Columbine—*Aquilegia canadensis*

Trailing Arbutus—*Epigaea repens*

Wake-Robin—*Trillium erectum*

Wild Pink—*Silene caroliniana*

By Cutting

White, Variable and Off-White, Green Tints

Bearberry—*Arctostaphylos uva-ursi*

Goldthread—*Coptis trifolia*

Partridgeberry—*Mitchella repens*

Wintergreen—*Gaultheria procumbens*

Clear Blue, Lavender, and Purple

Bellflower—*Campanula rapunculoides*

Wild Blue Phlox—*Phlox divaricata*

Wild Ginger—*Asarum canadense*

Pink, Purple-Red, and Red

Cardinal Flower—*Lobelia cardinalis*

Meadowsweet—*Spiraea latifolia*

Rugosa Rose—*Rosa rugosa*

Steeplebush—*Spiraea tomentosa*

Swamp Rose—*Rosa carolina*

Swamp Rose Mallow—*Hibiscus moscheutos*

Trailing Arbutus—*Epigaea repens*

101

WILD FLOWERS TO GROW

By Division

White, Variable and Off-White, Green Tints

Dutchman's-Breeches—*Dicentra cucullaria*

Pipsissewa—*Chimaphila umbellata*

Rattlesnake Plantain—*Epipactis tesselata*

Toothwort—*Dentaria diphylla*

Wild Calla—*Calla palustris*

Wood Sorrel—*Oxalis acetosella*

Clear Blue, Lavender, and Purple

Blue Flag—*Iris versicolor*

Common Violet—*Viola cucullata*

Crested Dwarf Iris—*Iris cristata*

Jack-in-the-Pulpit—*Arisaema triphyllum*

Spiderwort—*Tradescantia virginiana*

Virginia Cowslip—*Mertensia virginica*

Wild Bergamot—*Monarda fistulosa*

Yellow, Orange-Yellow, and Orange

Blue Cohosh—*Caulophyllum thalictroides*

Lady's-Slipper—*Cypripedium parviflorum*

Turk's-Cap Lily—*Lilium superbum*

Pink, Purple-Red, and Red

Moccasin Flower—*Cypripedium acaule*

Spring Beauty—*Claytonia virginica*

5. To Start a Woodland Garden

You can create a woodland garden almost anywhere. I know a charming one in a city backyard in Houston, Texas. Here a narrow flower-bordered walk leads among native trees and shrubs to a secluded spot where you can settle on an old log and breathe in the scent of woods. In contrast to the hum of cars from nearby, sun-warmed streets, this small oasis, with its trickle of water and deep shade, is cool and welcome.

Some years ago in a New York City suburb, we made another kind of woodland garden. It stretched along the north side of our boundary hedge, 40 feet long by 12 wide. A narrow walk curved among four hemlocks, three birches, and one pine. The short path turned so you could not see the end from the beginning. On either side bloomed Hepaticas, Bloodroot, Trillium, Violets, Dutchman's-Breeches, some golden Lady's-Slippers, and a wonderful clump of red-and-yellow Columbine. Here were weeks of spring enchantment; a place to wander by day or evening. Though of small area, it was woodland in essence, and a place of delight.

WILD FLOWERS TO GROW

In developing a wild flower area, you are in luck if your land includes a meadow, a bog, a woodlot, a stream, or a natural woods path. But there are great possibilities in your level, sunny 80 by 100-foot suburban backyard or 20 by 40-foot city lot. You most certainly can have woodland flowers.

A HOST OF SITES

Suitable locations for such a garden are: the shady side of a wall or hedge; under a large deep-rooted tree; under a few small trees; a shaded ledge; along the north house wall; and among thick shrubbery which can be pruned and shaped. Perhaps your garden area boasts not a single tree, and no other shade at all. Then your first step is to plant a tree, or two, or six. The best trees for starting a woodland or for increasing the amount of shade you already have are hemlock, pine, spruce, fir, beech, oak, and birch.

If you are in no hurry, a fascinating pastime is to start some trees from seed gathered along the roadside. Plant a handful of acorns, each an inch deep, and about 6 inches apart. By next year you will have a grove of 5-inch oaks. Every year they will grow a foot or more. A somewhat quicker method is to transplant tree seedlings from wild areas and roadsides. These may be moved in early spring or fall. Young birch, oak, pine, or hemlock will grow from 1 to 4 feet annually. (Remember that all land belongs to someone, and be sure to get permission first.) A still quicker procedure is to buy trees—10, 12, or 15 feet high. With a number of these and the help of your local nursery, you can create a young and promising woods in a single afternoon.

The six important growing conditions for woodland flowers are:

1. Excellent drainage
2. Protection from wind
3. Plenty of shade
4. Nearby water from faucet or rainbarrel (for you to apply in dry spells)
5. Soil that is slightly acid
6. Soil that is airy and friable.

Wild flowers do not thrive in packed earth, especially plants that spread and multiply by stems running underground. Where ground is hard and not at all like that in the woods, take out 18 inches of soil in the places you have marked for wild flowers. Remove intruding tree or shrub roots. Unless drainage is excellent, first refill the cavity with 2 inches of cinders, granite chips, or sharp sand. Next, shovel in 6 inches of the richest garden loam you have. On top of this spread a thin layer of equal parts superphosphate, ammonium sulphate, and powdered sulphur. This comprises an acid plant food, fine for a woods garden. Then add 6 inches of woodland compost, another thin layer of the plant food, plus half an inch of cotton-seed meal. Fill to the top with woods soil or compost. If woods soil is unavailable, peat moss may be substituted and mixed half and half with your richest earth.

If the place chosen for your wild flowers appears to have good drainage, and looks somewhat woodsy to start with, then a simpler way of preparing it will do. Merely turn over the soil to a depth of 6 inches, removing any roots. As you dig, incorporate a mixture of superphosphate, ammonium sulphate, and powdered sulphur. Also mix in about a half-inch of cottonseed meal and 3 inches of peat moss. Let this prepared soil settle two weeks before planting.

If your flower areas are few and small, there is a practical way of keeping out encroaching roots, and also helping to prevent the alkalizing of your acidified soil. A 9-inch-wide band of galvanized sheet metal, covered with rust-resistant paint, can be inserted around the edges, the upper rim just at soil level.

TO START A WOODLAND GARDEN

TREELESS SITES

I have seen a delightful group of woods flowers and ferns mingled for all-season attractiveness at the north corner of a house wall. Violets, Bloodroot, Dutchman's-Breeches, and Ferns enhance the area. The soil had been fairly rich and dark to start with so the spot had required little preparation.

Another fine place to start a woodland garden is at an outcropping of rock or a shaded rock ledge. Granite rock tends to acidify soil and provides ideal growing conditions. Artistically, a rock ledge is also a great asset. What alluring miniature heights and depths you have to work with. Small-scale ravines, earth pockets, depressions, delightful hillocks welcome all sorts of woods material. Ledges usually have excellent drainage, and offer numerous crevices and shelves for planting. The shallow soil there is ideal for many rock plants and Ferns. Sometimes water seeps down over the stone surface making the location compatible to still other varieties of wildings.

Building a woodland garden from the beginning may be compared with making a terrace, putting a new room on the house, or a bay window. It is a project that calls for basic construction. But then you have added some-

107

thing: a whole new dimension to your outdoors. Considered in this light, proper preparation at the start seems well worthwhile, and not too arduous.

A CAREFREE GARDEN

Once established, a woodland garden requires minimum care. In deep or even partial shade, few weeds grow. The plants, if they like the soil and location, will multiply and spread to cover the ground. A woods garden needs winter protection in the form of a mulch. Oak leaves are first choice because they give acidity to the soil, but whatever trees you have will probably drop their leaves to cover the area and save you the trouble.

Wild flowers planted in well-prepared soil seldom need feeding. Decomposing leaves usually provide ample supplies of nitrogen, phosphate, potash, and other elements. But you may lack ideal conditions and feel that your plants would benefit from additional food. Avoid cow manure, lime, and wood ashes. Instead, use pulverized hen, sheep, or horse manure adding, for each bucketful, two heaping tablespoons of powdered sulphur to create acidity. Spread this in midsummer.

Wildlings thrive in ground that is loose and soft. If your wild garden has no path, place several stepping stones about so you can walk through the planting without packing the earth. If possible, use weathered old stones, covered with lichen and moss, flat on one side and rounded on the other, and bury the rounded side. If you are to have a path, let it curve to offer some surprises— an artistic old stump, a great lichen-covered branch, a planting of your chosen flowers. Paths of pine and hemlock needles or of fine wood chips (from a tree-service company) discourage weeds and are pleasant to walk on. If your woods garden is closely associated with your lawn, make grass paths wide enough for convenient mowing.

There is something else you can do to accommodate your wild flowers and Ferns. In the forest, you will notice the debris scattered over the ground. This is beneficial to the plants there. It holds moisture, helps cool the earth in summer, warms it in winter, and provides an ideal medium for sprouting seeds or spreading roots. This ground litter is made up of decomposing pieces of bark and leaves. It includes small twigs, possibly disintegrating stumps, pine cones, and needles, fungi from fallen trees, lichen, dried moss, acorns, even hickory-nut shells, and a lot of other strange and wonderful items.

When you go out collecting, or anytime you drive into the country, put a basket in the car to hold such ground litter. Gather it where you can and spread it over your newly-made woods garden. As this debris decomposes, it furnishes life-giving humus. Meanwhile it brings a touch of the wild woodland to a suburban area.

The pleasures of a woodland garden do not depend on its size, but rather on choice material properly grown. Actually, the smaller the area the more opportunity you have to develop the appealing quality of intimacy. In a limited space with a limited amount of material you become more aware of individual plants. Each one comes into focus, and reveals its distinctive character and the details of its beauty. Regardless of how large or small your outdoor area is, don't hesitate to prepare somewhere for a few wild flowers.

TWENTY-SEVEN WOODLAND FLOWERS

White, Variable and Off-White, Green Tints

Bloodroot—*Sanguinaria canadensis*

Dutchman's-Breeches—*Dicentra cucullaria*

False-Solomon's Seal—*Smilacina racemosa*

Indian Pipe—*Monotropa uniflora*

Large Flowering Trillium—*Trillium grandiflorum*

May Apple—*Podophyllum peltatum*

Partridgeberry—*Mitchella repens*

Pipsissewa—*Chimaphila umbellata*

Rattlesnake Plantain—*Epipactis tesselata*

Solomon's-Seal—*Polygonatum biflorum*

Toothwort—*Dentaria diphylla*

Wild Lily-of-the-Valley—*Maianthemum canadense*

110

TO START A WOODLAND GARDEN

Clear Blue, Lavender, and Purple

Common Violet—*Viola cucullata*
Fringed Gentian—*Gentiana crinita*

Jack-in-the-Pulpit—*Arisaema triphyllum*
Lupine—*Lupinus perennis*
Wild Ginger—*Asarum canadense*

Yellow, Orange-Yellow, and Orange

Bellwort—*Uvularia sessilifolia*
Dog's-Tooth Violet—*Erythronium americanum*

Jewelweed—*Impatient biflora*
Lady's-Slipper—*Cypripedium parviflorum*

Pink, Purple-Red, and Red

Columbine—*Aquilegia canadensis*
Moccasin Flower—*Cypripedium acaule*
Pinesap—*Monotropa hypopitys*

Spring Beauty—*Claytonia virginica*
Trailing Arbutus—*Epigaea repens*
Wake-Robin—*Trillium erectum*

6. Plants for a Spring Picture

Spring splashes and sprays the hillsides with a special kind of green. A rosy glow spreads over tree tops. Warming days gild the willows and waken little creatures sleeping in our stone walls. Spring stirs a desire to get outdoors and wander. It is a restlessness—almost a fever.

And spring is Hepaticas. Up through the rich black forest floor they come. These first blooms emerge from a nest of furry buds. The 1-inch flowers on 4- to 6-inch stems are deep blue with white stamens, also rosy lavender, or white. With a wide-eyed look they greet the newborn season. Last year's olive-green three-lobed leaves survive the winter to contrast with the first fresh flowers. After blossoms fade, old foliage withers and new green leaves unfold. Flower buds, stems, and leaves are downy or hairy—perhaps for warmth while nights are cold and frost still comes.

Hepaticas (*Hepatica triloba*) transplant readily to the garden. In the wild they grow on shady hillsides and will thrive along a north house wall, under tall trees, or under one tree, on dry rocky slopes or banks, among oaks and

112

beech. They need a winter cover, if possible of oak or beech leaves. Remove these in March and flowers soon appear. A moderately acid to neutral soil rich in humus is ideal, and the best time to transplant, immediately after flowering. Good companion plants are Bloodroot, Jack-in-the-Pulpit, Violets, Solomon's-Seal, and Wild Columbine. Together these provide blossoms from early April through May.

QUEEN FOR A DAY

Bloodroot (*Sanguinaria canadensis*) sends up a single bud wrapped in a protective green leaf. As the bud becomes a flower, the leaf gradually unfurls. The pure white blossom stands 10 inches above last year's leaves and resembles a small Water Lily. There are usually eight slim and tapering petals that open out flat each morning, rise up at noon, and fold at dusk. When the bloom is over and petals fall, the leaf stands flat and large, umbrella-style, a guard for the long brown seed capsule at its center.

The sap from a broken root of this plant is blood red, hence the name. Indians used this root-juice for dye. An oldtime remedy for coughs was this red juice on a lump of sugar.

Bloodroot borders shady back roads and sweeps through

open woods. An adaptable flower, it thrives in rich neutral or slightly acid soil. It must have partial shade, average moisture, and a winter covering of leaves (again, oak or beech are best). Transplant clumps in early fall. At this time they are easy to locate because of the single leaf at the top of every stalk, each with three or more indentations. The seeds may be sown as soon as ripe. They will germinate the next spring and bloom a year later. Our Bloodroot grows on a rocky, western, partly shaded slope next to a low retaining wall of field stone. Thriving nearby are Wild Columbine, Hepaticas, Solomon's-Seal, Wild Bleeding Heart, Toothwort, Royal Ferns, Jewelweed, and Virginia Bluebells.

DAINTY TUBER

Spring Beauty (*Claytonia virginica*) grows from a tiny tuber. The five-petaled pale pink blossoms are one-half inch to one inch across, and in clusters. Petals are lined with dark pink veins, and the blossoms have a touch of gold in the center. The flowers on 5- to 7-inch stems rise from the midst of grasslike foliage. Never pick for flowers and leaves share the same stalk, and there will not be enough foliage left to support the plant. After seed ripens, the whole plant disappears for the season. Provide a winter cover of oak and beech leaves.

Spring Beauties thrive in the high shade of deciduous woods in deep rich leaf mold, and preferably in moist areas. Actually they will adapt to various soils, and do well in moderately acid soil. When you transplant, take a large clump of earth with each plant and firm the corns into the soil so they are 3 inches deep. This delicate little flower, opening so early in the spring, is host to countless bees and butterflies.

Two Dicentras

Dutchman's-Breeches (*Dicentra cucullaria*) sends up fine-cut, fernlike leaves at the first hint of spring. In April or May, white flowers with yellow touches unfold, three to seven on a stem. Each floret resembles a pair of small Dutch pantaloons. Our Dutchman's-Breeches are rapidly spreading up and down the west stony bank of the stream where, coming and going for three weeks or more, they fill the area with bloom. After the flowers pass, the foliage is lovely for many subsequent weeks.

Before summer, seed capsules, like small pea pods, open to spread their bounty. Ideal conditions for Dutchman's-Breeches are open woods, somewhat damp, and slightly acid or neutral soil with plenty of humus. They thrive on rocky eastern or western slopes. By midsummer the plant disappears, but do not be concerned for it will return next spring.

Wild Bleeding Heart (*Dicentra eximia*) has delicate pink heart-shaped blossoms, several florets to a stem. These emerge from feathery foliage in May, and the plant continues flowering off and on until September. It thrives in open shade, in rich humusy woods soil which is moderately acid. The roots have a wandering habit, and the six plants you set out will, in a year or two, become twelve, then twenty-four, and on and on. You will find that sweeps of these delightful flowers grow rampantly enough to crowd out even Pachysandra. Rarely is Wild Bleeding Heart disturbed by insects or disease. This is one of the easiest flowers to grow, and one of the hardiest; hence it is a must for any woodland area.

VIOLETS AND WAKE-ROBINS

The family of Violets is a large and illustrious one. There is the Common Violet (*Viola cucullata*) which you find everywhere, and the Sweet White Violet (*Viola blanda*) which has a lovely scent and grows in dry woodlands as well as wet meadows. The Yellow Violet (*Viola pubescens*) is pale gold and grows to 12 inches with branching, forked stems. It thrives in thickets or moist woodland areas.

Violets grow in light shade, in woodland borders, in a mulch of fallen leaves. They also thrive in the full sun of our vegetable gardens, which shows their adaptability. Except for the Bird's-Foot, the Yellow, and the Canada Violets, these are woodland flowers you can pick with no harm to plant or bloom. They make charming boutonnieres, are pretty in your hair, and can fill your house with miniature bouquets—you can also eat the extra ones! In early spring young Violet leaves enhance a salad. Try some of the petals in white-bread sandwiches with Watercress. They are not only delicious but also quite a conversation piece at a luncheon party. Violets are tough and hardy, and once started will spread and thrive. They reproduce by seed and by division of roots.

Trillium (*Trillium grandiflorum*) is one of spring's loveliest and most valued blossoms. Throughout Ohio and many of the midwestern states it grows by the acre, and it will spread for you, too, in an astonishing manner. Each pure white 10-inch-high bloom has three petals and three sepals. The blossom rises above three light green veined leaves and lasts for several weeks. As flowers mature, the petals turn pink. The seeds, 1-inch red berries, form in late summer and are also decorative.

Officially, Trillium grows in rich moist woods, in acid soil, and in the shade of high deciduous trees. It also flour-

117

ishes in evergreen woods, along open roadsides, in thickets, ravines, and on wooded slopes. But Trillium is a flower with a streak of the rebel in it. You never know what any one plant will do until you try it. I once planted a Trillium in a sunny perennial border. The soil was rich and filled with humus, but no tree shaded the area. This Trillium flourished, and the flowers were huge and long lasting. The plant multiplied.

There is also a handsome Red Trillium, the common Wake-Robin or Birthroot (*Trillium erectum*). The flower, while similar to the white variety, is smaller, and the open blossom nods a little. Christmas Ferns, Lady Ferns, and Solomon's-Seal naturalize well with red and white Trilliums in a woodland.

Spring Slippers

Moccasin Flower or pink Lady's-Slipper (*Cypridedium acaule*) is one of the finest spring flowers. Early in the season a pair of light green leaves appear, large and gracefully rounded, ribbed and lined. From the center of each pair a single, slightly fragrant flower rises on a 10-inch stem. The bud unopened is a symphony of enchanting curves. When unfolded it reveals a crimson-pink pouch surrounded by wavy brown sepals and petals. It remains in flower for weeks.

118

The pink Lady's-Slipper grows in dry woodland, near pines, and also in moist, partially shaded deciduous woods beneath oaks and beeches, but not with evergreens. For success an acid soil is needed. Lady's-Slippers are tricky to move and to grow. Be sure to get all the roots; they forage deeper than you think. They will be happiest if you take plenty of soil from their original site and provide a winter covering of oak leaves. They spread by underground roots and, if grown in their choice of earth and location, may well multiply. Too often the transplanted Moccasin Flower thrives for a year or two and then just disappears. Perhaps the best way to establish, and thus to save them, is to buy a few plants from a local nursery. Never, never pick a Lady's-Slipper. If you do, the plant will die.

The yellow Lady's-Slipper is more adaptable. Usually it flourishes even in ordinary garden loam or in woodland soil that is moderately acid. Once established, it thrives for years and years and spreads in a location that has proved pleasing.

TASTY ROOT AND TRAILING ARBUTUS

Toothwort or Crinkleroot (*Dentaria diphylla*) is named for its long fleshy, wrinkled root with teethlike scales. The root tastes like Watercress or Horseradish. Its tangy flavor is delicious in bread-and-butter sandwiches. The four-petaled, 10-inch-high flowers are less than an inch in diameter and have yellow stamens; they are grouped in clusters. During May they transform the area where they grow into drifts of white foam. The prettily cut leaves are three lobed and tooth edged. You will discover the plants in the semishade of high trees, at the top of banks, along roadsides. They flower before the trees leaf out. After blooming the plants die down and disappear until next season.

Trailing Arbutus (*Epigaea repens*) is a prima donna among wild flowers—beautiful and tantalizing—so appealing and so hard to grow. The bloom is fresh and fragrant, with an unsophisticated charm. The plant is hairy stemmed, the leaves 1 to 4 inches long. New leaves, which develop in early summer, are an attractive pinkish brown.

Pink-tinted white flowers form in clusters, each cluster at the end of a trailing stem. Arbutus sprawls over rocks, ledges, or banks and grows on high hillsides or mountains. It thrives under pine and oak, in half or full shade. Give the plant rich, sandy, rocky, very acid soil, and a well-drained location.

Arbutus is difficult to transplant, partly because of the long trailing stems. Move only small plants with plenty of sod. Since the plant is on conservation lists in most states, you will probably have to buy it. Or you can gather seeds and experiment. Trailing Arbutus should be watered lightly in a drought and given a winter cover of pine needles. I've seen banksides of this lovely spring flower in the mountains of North Carolina as well as in the Connecticut woods. Wherever Arbutus grows, in spring its scent announces its whereabouts long before you see it. Then when you do come upon it, the waxy flowers and fresh spring fragrance make you tarry in admiration.

UNINVITED BUT WELCOME

Shooting Star (*Dodecatheon meadia*), sometimes called Indian Chief or American Cowslip, arrived by itself in our meadow. Part of the charm of wild flowers is that they sometimes do this. The unusual little flower on a 1-foot stalk comes in magenta, pink, or white. Florets are in clusters. Petals are sharply reflexed and stamens point downward, giving the effect of a shooting star heading for earth. This plant thrives in open woods, on hillsides, and in stony ground. Actually it can adapt to many soils and grows in partial sun or shade. The four to six leaves form beguiling rosettes on the ground. It thrives in a very acid or moderately acid soil. Give it a light winter cover.

Wild Columbine (*Aquilegia canadensis*) has a delicate,

nodding scarlet flower with yellow touches. It thrives in semishade along the north side of our stone wall. It can adapt to almost any soil and to either sun or shade. I've also seen Columbine flourishing in an open sunny field on Putney Mountain, Vermont. Deep roots enable the plant to survive drought. Rocky Mountain Columbine (*Aquilegia caerulea*) is the State Flower of Colorado. The 4-inch blooms are blue and white. This one will thrive east of the Rockies if you provide a very acid soil. It can be bought from nurseries.

Wild Geranium or Cranesbill (*Geranium maculatum*) sweeps over the Swiss Alps. There the flowers are deep violet-blue. In our Connecticut woodland, they are paler but equally lovely. Individual flowers are 1 to 1½ inches across. They reseed readily and will bloom in almost any soil, from very acid to neutral. The deeply cut leaves are soft and flexible. Stems are hairy, and unfolding flowers are covered with silver down.

Crested Dwarf Iris (*Iris cristata*) is a lovely little 5-inch plant with light violet blooms and yellow centers. It thrives in half sun and half shade where it spangles May hillsides with color and subtle fragrance. Dwarf Iris (*Iris verna*) is but 3 inches high and, if given extremely acid soil, grows into thick mats of bloom. This one is intense lavender-blue with brilliant gold at the petal base. Both sorts spread in great sweeps through the Smoky Mountains and do equally well in Connecticut woods.

Of all the wild flowers mentioned here the only kinds to pick are the Violets, with those exceptions noted above.

In general, all these plants thrive in the high shade of deciduous woods and are especially happy near oak and beech. Each has preferences: the particular conditions that give it extra health and vigor. Many will adapt to conditions that are similar, if not identical, to those of their native homes. Your best course is to approximate as nearly as possible their choices, and then wait and see what happens. But once in a while, you will want to experiment as we did with our Trillium in the perennial border.

After a long winter—and by the time spring comes, all winters seem to have been long—we warmly welcome our woodland flowers. We greet them with joy as they fill our shady areas with their delightfully subtle scents, their lovely forms and colors, and their interesting personalities. Try as many as you have space for, and maybe a few more. Here is a Baker's Dozen to choose from:

Bellwort—*Uvularia sessilifolia*
Blue Cohosh—*Caulophyllum thalictroides*
Bunchberry—*Cornus canadensis*
False Solomon's-Seal—*Smilacina racemosa*

WILD FLOWERS TO GROW

Goldthread—*Coptis trifolia*
Jack-in-the-Pulpit—*Arisaema triphyllum*
May Apple—*Podophyllum peltatum*
Partridgeberry—*Mitchella repens*
Pipsissewa—*Chimaphila umbellata*
Solomon's-Seal—*Polygonatum biflorum*
Wild Ginger—*Asarum canadense*
Wild Lily-of-the-Valley—*Maianthemum canadense*
Wood Anemone—*Anemone quinquefolia*

7. A Garden by the Sea

The ocean is blue, the sky is blue—sometimes you cannot tell where one ends and the other begins. The sand is white-gold. The gulls are calling, waves breaking, and salty breezes blowing. Against such a backdrop of wide-open spaces, of a landscape completely horizontal, you can have a fascinating array of wild flowers.

Some flowers grow in pure white sand—among them Rugosa Roses and Dusty Miller. Others grow on sunny bluffs a short distance above the sea in soil so light and warm to touch it seems to be all sand; these include Bearberry, Bird's-Foot Violet, and Chicory. Along marshes, inlets, and near brackish water, you'll find Sea Lavender and Rose Mallow. Windblown pines and scrub-oak woods, where mittenlike Sassafras leaves turn gold in autumn, are host to Sweet Fern, Indian Pipes, Lupine, and many more. Most of the plants are yours for the digging, but again, to be doubly sure, check the conservation list in Chapter 16 or that of your own state.

Beginning in May with Scotch Broom, through a summer of Wild Roses and Beach Plums, into Goldenrod and Aster time, there is a seaside procession of flowers, shrubs, grasses, and trees as well for background.

A SUITABLE LAWN

Suppose your seaside house is surrounded more by sand than soil. Or maybe just by pure sand. Suppose the sand blows under the door and into the dinner, and gets in your hair. *And* you want a lawn. You could bulldoze off a layer of sand, buy topsoil and good grass seed, apply fertilizer, and reseed a number of times. But there is a simpler solution.

Have you ever watched Beachgrass swirling in the breeze, creating lovely interlocking circles in the sand? Do you know how easy it is to bring this whole process up near your front door, to anchor the sandy soil where it belongs? A lawn of Beachgrass may be a new concept but it is a lawn that never needs cutting, weeding, or feeding. It is not only unusual and beautiful, but also it costs nothing.

Beachgrass is officially called *Ammophila,* from the Greek words meaning "sand" and "love"; *Arenaria* is the variety to use. In early spring or fall, partially dig up a number of Beachgrass clumps with 4-inch pieces of root. Bring the clumps home, and bury the roots 4 inches, setting the clumps 6 inches apart. Do not plant too solidly, but arrange the roots in drifts with sand spaces between, as you probably found them growing. Leave a place for a walk and a few areas for flowers and bushes. Let the grass spread in waves, conforming to contours of the land; thus you bring into closer proximity, for greater appreciation, the curve of distant dunes and graceful shore line.

Beachgrass grows about 2 feet high, is tough and hardy, doesn't mind a bath of salt spray at times, and is guaranteed to keep banks and dunes from shifting about in storms. The slim arching blades not only sketch patterns in the sand as they bend and drift with the wind, but, like the sea itself, they are never still. You seldom tire of watching them ripple. In summer the tall, straight seed pods turn gold in the sunlight and can make interesting additions to winter bouquets.

BUSHES ON THE BEACH

Three bushes for the sandy garden that will form a low hedge, a background for flowers, or focal points in the overall composition are Bayberry, Beach Plum, and Rugosa Roses. On Cape Cod I have seen all three growing naturally along the edges of the beach.

Bayberry is a sturdy shrub that grows up to 5 feet high, but can be kept to any desired height by rigorous pruning. It spreads by underground runners and eventually forms a thick hedgelike growth. It makes an attractive property-line marker, and is an interesting accent anywhere. An added bonus is the goldfinches and warblers that will nest in it. Crush a Bayberry leaf for its pungent scent. The purple metallic sheen of the fall foliage adds to its decorative value. Silver-gray berries appearing in late summer transform the stiff branches into material for indoor winter arrangements. On Cape Cod is the center of the Bayberry candle industry. Watching the great wheel of wicks being dipped in and out of a caldron of melted Bayberry wax and gradually becoming candles may inspire you to make your own. (We tell you how in Chapter 12.) The candles smell so nice, too, when burning.

The ideal time to move Bayberry is in early spring or late fall. Take as much root as possible and don't worry if tops straggle. Trim them to the ground and fresh plants will emerge with leaves thickly settled over the stalks.

When I first transplanted Beach Plum to our place on Cape Cod, I was, and still am, convinced that there is one main Beach Plum root up in Sandwich somewhere from which all others stem. The best way to assure success in transplanting is to try to find a plant apart from a cluster—if you can.

Beach Plum has jet-black, stiff, angular stems. First, in

May come tight little buds like white beads on a string. These open into a snowstorm of flowers. They mature to an appealing pink. In midsummer the plums ripen purple, and then the fun begins. Beach Plum jelly is a joy— fun and easy to make, fine for gifts as well as for your own shelves.

TALE OF A ROSE

There is an interesting story about how the Rugosa Rose first came to Cape Cod. More than a century ago, a Japanese ship loaded with young plants was wrecked off the coast. After floating in the sea and being roughly rolled to shore, the plants took hold in the sand and spread. Today we find the Rugosa Rose prospering everywhere. What plant could have more lust for life?

You discover the pink or white Rugosa Roses flowering in hot, dry beach sand, spreading their scent far and wide. In sunlight, in fog, after a rain, anytime in June, and almost anywhere along the coast, you encounter this deep rich fragrance. The blossoms last wonderfully well indoors and scent the whole house. In autumn the plant is covered with orange hips that make a delicious jam, and are valuable nutritionally for their high proportion of vitamin C.

WILD FLOWERS TO GROW

GAY QUARTET

Four colorful flowers to group here and there in the foreground of a seaside border are Beach Pea, Dusty Miller, False Heather, and Goldenrod. Beach Pea (*Lathyrus maritimus*), a luxurious vinelike plant, not only survives, but burgeons in soil that appears quite sterile. Rosy purple flowers open continuously for weeks during the summer, and the silver-down pods that follow are as decorative as the curling tendrils terminating each leaf-stalk. Both stems and flowers add greatly to floral arrangements. The Beach Pea ranges widely from the Oregon coast southward to California and from Maine to Florida. It also thrives in Greenland, the Aleutians, and Japan.

In contrast to the rich blue-green foliage of the Beach Pea is the silver-gray Dusty Miller (*Artemisia stelleriana*). The modest yellow flower, rising tall and straight from the midst of wool-lace leaves lasts from June to September. The charm of the plant lies mainly in the gray foliage that turns to silver in fog or dew. This is an easy wildling to transplant *if* you get the whole of the root.

False Heather (*Hudsonia tomentosa*) is intriguing. On its stiff angular branches the small leaves seem to grow one out of the other. On sunny days in June and July, tiny flowers transform the plant into a sheet of gold. This fine ground cover was probably pushed down by glaciers in the Ice Age, so it has an interesting past as well as present charms. To discover the intricate detail of the blossoms, look through a magnifying glass.

In late August several kinds of Goldenrod bloom at the shore. One of the loveliest is the Seaside Goldenrod (*Solidago sempervirens*). This grows 18 inches to 4 feet tall with substantial smooth-edged leaves and gold flowers as bright as the sunlight in which they flourish. Each branching stalk is packed with golden florets. The rich flamboyant blossoms bring sunshine to the beach even on cloudy days.

Now move back from the very sandy areas to the top of the bluffs above the beach. While the soil here is not quite so sandy it still seems hopelessly light and infertile. Yet the plants just mentioned will thrive here and a number of others as well. And then as you step under pines into the woods, still more doors open. Along inlets and ponds and sunny bogs more material is available to you.

What will grow on your seaside land? Much depends on your type of soil and on other factors. Do you have very sandy land? Or gray-brown sandy soil, light and blowy, or maybe rocky? Woods? A bog or a pond? An inlet

131

or shoreline? The lists at the end of this chapter will help you select the right plant for your particular location. There are many possibilities for each area.

On Timing

The preferred time to transplant seaside plants and shrubs is early spring or late fall. But you can succeed even in midsummer, if you are intuitive about weather and do the job just before a rain. The third day of a nor'easter, when you are tired of staying indoors, is a perfect time to move wild plants and bushes.

To see and know well a number of native flowers you would have to range far and wide. But in your seashore garden they are telescoped into closer association both with each other and with you. Before starting you should have a pretty good plan in mind. The idea is not to have a scraggly garden that looks neglected by man, but to create an area near your house that suggests the atmosphere and poetry of the seashore before man began to deal with it. Such a garden depends for charm not on the symmetry of well-marked beds and paths, but rather on sweeps of Beachgrass, clumps of Dusty Miller, and drifts of Beach Pea. Let the design appear as casual as the surrounding wildness.

The woodland garden rule about observing, and then

duplicating, native conditions is equally applicable to seaside wild gardens. This rule isn't too difficult to practice with collected or purchased specimens, because many varieties, you soon discover, will adapt to more than one location.

To Transplant Successfully

Why are so many seashore plants able to survive lashing winter storms and thrive weeks on end in summer with never a drop of rain, in what appears to be pure sand? A major reason is that these plants send roots unbelievably far down. Thus, the points of success in transplanting a seashore plant are:

(1) Be sure to get all the roots of each plant.
(2) Choose plants that are relatively small. (It is easier to get all the roots of a small plant, and a small plant also adjusts more readily.)
(3) When possible, select plants that grow apart from the parent.

After the move keep replanted material well watered for days until the foliage has regained vigor and stiffness, and you can see that the plant has taken hold.

Further Features

A path adds a pleasant note to any garden, especially one at the seashore. You might make it of smooth, round, white pebbles collected on the beach; they shimmer brightly in the rain. You can save shells from clambakes and crush them, or crush oyster shells. Additional features might include larger shells, and a few interesting stones gathered along the shore to introduce beauty of color and shape, a piece of gray, sculptured driftwood, a weathered log for sunset-viewing. Fishnet, pulleys, buoys, rusty anchors, and the like should be used with restraint in your garden plan lest you end up looking like Ye Olde Tyme Gifte Shoppe.

The only care involved in this kind of garden is to keep things pruned to scale within the original plan, and perhaps to improve the composition with a few additions from time to time, as the spirit moves.

So if you live at the shore, instead of overhauling your landscape or trying to coax standard annuals and perennials to grow there, try this more carefree approach. Not only is such a pleasant line of least resistance in keeping with lazy summer days, but actually you will be creating an unusual and distinctive garden, one as rewarding as it is easy.

A seashore house surrounded by seashore plants merges wonderfully with the landscape. There is such a rightness about these flowers growing in their proper soil and location. They have the vigor of perfect health which in itself is beauty.

Once you start planning such a garden every coastal back road issues a tempting invitation. And a rainy day at the shore changes from liability to opportunity. Rain or shine, you find yourself observing with increased insight not only the whys and wherefores of plants as they grow, but all of nature around you. Soon you are deep in new and wonderful realms.

PLANTS FOR SEASIDE GARDENING

TREES

Hickory, Mockernut	*Carya glabra*	Dry woods
Shagbark	*ovata*	Rich boggy areas or dry woods, bottom lands, slopes
Maple, Sycamore	*Acer pseudo-platanus*	Dry woods
Oak, Black	*Quercus velutina*	Dry gravelly land
Post	*stellata*	Woods, shore, dry sandy hills
Scrub	*ilicifolia*	Sandy barrens, rocky soil
Pine, Austrian	*Pinus nigra*	Dry woods, open land
Pitch	*rigida*	Dry sandy soil, swamps

135

WILD FLOWERS TO GROW

Scotch	*sylvestris*	Barren sandy soil
Sassafras	*Sassafras albidum*	Rich woods
Sour Gum	*Nyssa sylvatica*	Swampy woods, edge of bogs

SHRUBS

Bayberry	*Myrica caroliniensis*	Sand, hot and dry meadows, open woods
Beach Plum	*Prunus maritima*	Sand, sunny dry meadows, roadsides, shoreland
Blueberry, Dwarf	*Vaccinium caespitosum*	Hot, dry, rocky ground
Low	*pennsylvanicum*	Dry hills, rocky soil
Rabbit's-Eye	*virgatum*	Woodland, swamps, dry thickets
Chokeberry	*Pyrus arbutifolia*	Boggy woods
Hawthorn	*Crataegus intricata*	Thickets and open woods
Hazelnut	*Corylus americana*	Hedgerows, thickets
Huckleberry	*Gaylussacia baccata*	Rocky woods and thickets
Inkberry	*Ilex glabra*	Sandy coastal flats
Juniper, Common	*Juniperus communis*	Dry hillsides and rocky pastures
Creeping	*horizontalis*	Rocky, sandy areas, swamp edges
Rugosa Rose	*Rosa rugosa*	Dry sandy, sunny areas, meadows

Sand Myrtle	*Leiophyllum buxi-folium*	Sandy barrens
Shadbush	*Amelanchier canadensis*	Hillsides, open woodland
Stagger Bush	*Lyonia mariana*	Low, sandy coastal areas
Sweet Fern	*Comptonia asplenifolia*	Stony fields, sandy banks, dry pastures
Sweet Pepperbush	*Clethra alnifolia*	Moist woods, shores of fresh ponds

GRASS AND VINES

Beach-Grass	*Ammophila arenaria*	Pure sand
Clematis, Virgin's-Bower	*Clematis virginiana*	Bog and dry meadow
Climbing Wild Cucumber	*Echinocystis lobata*	Bog
Grape, Northern Fox	*Vitis labrusca*	Wet and dry thickets, woods-edge
Virginia Creeper	*Parthenocissus quinquefolia*	Woods, sandy rocky banks

FLOWERS

The flowers are divided into four color groups. Their locations are indicated by these five key letters: B- Bog, wet pasture, pond edge, or in the water; I Inlet or shore; L Light sandy soil, sunny meadow; S Almost pure sand; W Fringe woodland

WILD FLOWERS TO GROW

White, Variable and Off-White, Green Tints

Beach Clotbur	*Xanthium echinatum*	L
Bearberry	*Arctostaphylos uva-ursi*	L
Bladder Campion	*Silene latifolia*	L
Bunchberry	*Cornus canadensis*	W
Daisy Fleabane	*Erigeron ramosus*	L
Evening Lychnis	*Lychnis alba*	L
Hedge Bindweed	*Convolvulus sepium*	B
Indian Pipe	*Monotropa uniflora*	W
Marsh Trefoil	*Menyanthes trifoliata*	B
Michaelmas Daisy	*Aster ericoides*	L
Oxeye-Eye-Daisy	*Chrysanthemum leucanthemum*	L
Partridgeberry	*Mitchella repens*	W
Pearly Everlasting	*Anaphalis margaritacea*	L
Pipsissewa	*Chimaphila umbellata*	W
Queen Anne's Lace	*Daucus carota*	L
Sweet White Violet	*Viola blanda*	W, B
Tall Meadow Rue	*Thalictrum polygamum*	B
White Water Lily	*Nymphaea odorata*	B
Wild Calla	*Calla palustris*	B
Wintergreen	*Gaultheria procumbens*	W
Yarrow	*Achillea millefolium*	L
Yucca	*Hespero-Yucca whipplei*	L

Clear Blue, Lavender, and Purple

Asiatic Dayflower	*Commelina communis*	L, W
Bird's-Foot Violet	*Viola pedata*	L, W
Blue-eyed Grass	*Sisyrinchium angustifolium*	W, L
Blunt-leaved Milkweed	*Asclepias amplexicaulis*	S, L

138

Bottle Gentian	*Gentiana andrewsi*	W
Chicory	*Cichorium intybus*	S, L
Common Milkweed	*Asclepias syriaca*	S, L
Common Violet	*Viola cucullata*	W, B
Jack-in-the-Pulpit	*Arisaema triphyllum*	W
Lupine	*Lupinus perennis*	W
Marsh Rosemary	*Limonium carolinianum*	S, I
New England Aster	*Aster novae-angliae*	L
Nightshade	*Solanum dulcamara*	W
Pickerelweed	*Pontederia cordata*	B
Purple Coneflower	*Brauneria purpurea*	L
Red Clover	*Trifolium pratense*	L
Wild Geranium	*Geranium maculatum*	W

Yellow, Orange-Yellow, and Orange

Black-eyed Susan	*Rudbeckia hirta*	L
Bush Honeysuckle	*Diervilla lonicera*	W, L
Butter-and-Eggs	*Linaria vulgaris*	L
Buttercup	*Ranunculus acris*	L, W
Butterfly Weed	*Asclepias tuberosa*	L
Dandelion	*Taraxacum officinale*	L
Day Lily	*Hemerocallis fulva*	W, L
Devil's-Paintbrush	*Hieracium canadense*	W, L
Downy False Foxglove	*Gerardia flava*	W, L
Dusty Miller	*Artemisia stelleriana*	S, L
False Heather	*Hudsonia tomentosa*	I, S
Five-Finger	*Potentilla canadensis*	L, W
Goldenrod	*Solidago* sp.	L, S
Great Mullein	*Verbascum thapsus*	S, L
Star Grass	*Hypoxis hirsuta*	L
Sunflower	*Helianthus giganteus*	L, W

WILD FLOWERS TO GROW

Turk's-Cap Lily	*Lilium superbum*	L
Yellow Pond Lily	*Nymphaea advena*	B

Pink, Purple-Red, and Red

Beach Pea	*Lathyrus maritimus*	S, L
Coast Jointweed	*Polygonella articulata*	S, I
Common Thistle	*Cirsium lanceolatum*	S, I, L
Fireweed	*Epilobium angustifolium*	L, W
Joe-Pye Weed	*Eupatorium purpureum*	W, B, L
Lady's-Thumb	*Polygonum persicaria*	L, B
Milkwort	*Polygala sanguinea*	L, B
Moccasin Flower	*Cypripedium acaule*	B, W
Pinesap	*Monotropa hypopitys*	W
Swamp Rose	*Rosa carolina*	B, L
Swamp Rose Mallow	*Hibiscus moscheutos*	L, B

8. A Wild Garden in Deep Shade

Suppose you have a corner of dense shade. A number of early spring flowers and a few summer ones will thrive where scarcely a beam of sunlight penetrates. Here you may design and plant a cool and inviting retreat, a place of peace and quiet.

Except for Indian Pipe and Pinesap, most shade-tolerant species also grow beneath high deciduous trees where they get sun before the leaves open in spring and again in autumn after leaves have fallen. Many of these species flourish along streams and stone walls in filtered sun. But the great value of these plants is that they bloom—in heavy shade. I have discovered fourteen that are reliable for the dark corners.

As with other woodland areas, a thickly shaded spot must have thorough soil preparation. Dig down a spade's depth and remove roots. If the soil is firmly packed, incorporate a 5-inch layer of compost, humus, woods soil, or peat moss.

One of my favorite plants for deep shade is Jack-in-the-Pulpit (*Arisaema triphyllum*). The striped sheath is the pulpit from which Jack preaches. Aside from the charm of name and color pattern, this plant has an unusual way of life. The small, well-concealed flower parts in all young plants are male. In two to five years, the same plant turns into a female, and the flowers are fertile. However, if conditions are not favorable, blossoms remain male indefinitely, and the plants do not multiply.

In August and September, bright red berries appear. A good time to transplant is soon after the berries have been eaten by the local wildlife. Jack-in-the-Pulpit flourishes in acid soil. When digging, try to get *all* the 8- to 12-inch roots. When setting out a plant, let the roots go just as deep. The stem will need a firm support of soil around it.

FORCING JACKS

There is something intriguing that you can do with a few of your Jack-in-the-Pulpit corms after plants are well established, and if you have an ample number; it's called forcing. In the fall, fill a large flower pot (6 inches or more deep) with rich woods soil; plant three to five corms 1 inch apart and about 4 inches deep. Sink the container outdoors in the ground. Cover with leaves and burlap to prevent solid freezing. Dig up and bring the pot into the house after Christmas. Within a few weeks, you will have small-scale Jack-in-the-Pulpits to decorate your living room. While they do not attain full size, they create the atmosphere of spring woods several months ahead of time. When weather permits, put them back in the garden where the plants will adjust again to outdoor living.

That early-spring day you explore the woods for the first Hepaticas, you will probably also discover Wild Ginger (*Asarum canadense*) in flower. Monkey Jugs is the North Carolina name for the little vase-shaped blooms snuggled deep in the heart of the plant. This is a blossom to seek out, for it is well hidden beneath chocolate-brown, furry, indented leaves.

Since Wild Ginger spreads by rootstock, it is difficult to tell where one plant ends and the next begins. The root's strong gingery scent is responsible for the name. The small brown blooms remain on the plant for weeks and change little even after seed pods have formed, for these develop within the flower. Wild Ginger thrives in rich, loose, moist loam. It makes an excellent ground cover for woodland gardens because when other foliage disappears, the leaves of Wild Ginger keep an area invitingly green. Wild Ginger does well with ferns under shrubbery, but always in deep shade. In thick woods I have seen a veritable blanket of plants transforming a large gray rock into a mound of green.

SOLOMON'S-SEAL AND BLUE COHOSH

False Solomon's-Seal (*Smilacina racemosa*), sometimes called Solomon's-Plume, is ideal for the north or west side of stone walls. It will grow in rocky areas and in the shadow of tall trees. The oval leaves alternate up the stem. Diminutive, foamy white flowers develop at the top of each stalk. For dim corners, under heavy foliage, this flower is a white delight. In the fall the green, lined leaves turn golden chartreuse, and above them a bunch of red berries is a bright accent.

Common Solomon's-Seal (*Polygonatum biflorum*) is a similar plant, but the flowers are different, and differently arranged. Under every pair of leaves all the way up the arching· stalk, twin blossoms swing, each a small, flared white bell. The plant is easy to grow and will thrive in almost any soil, provided there is a little moisture. It flourishes in a rocky area or in deep leaf mold. In autumn when the leaves are a transluscent yellow, blue-black berries decorate the plant.

Blue Cohosh or Papoose Root (*Caulophyllum thalictroides*), in spite of its name, has no blue flowers, but greenish yellow ones. The blueness lies in the first gently curving spring-stems as they emerge from the ground. When the lacy leaves open, they also have a bluish cast. A final blueness appears in the attractive fall berries. The plant thrives in deep shade and humus-filled soil, slightly moist. It will grow in places where few other things live and delights in forest shadows. Good companion plants include Solomon's-Seal, Jack-in-the-Pulpit, and May Apple.

SPRING UMBRELLA

The May Apple (*Podophyllum peltatum*) emerges from the forest floor like a folded green umbrella. The single stalk reaches a foot or more in height, and then the umbrella unfolds. On a stem, poised at a fork between two umbrella leaves, is a delightful, waxy white six-petaled flower with a central dot of yellow. The leaves may broaden to 9 inches, and are deeply cut and indented. A cluster of May apples brings the first note of bright green to the spring woods.

May Apples grow close together and, when the leaves are fully open, they hide the ground. While the foliage is poisonous, the fruit is an edible berry, tasting rather like an insipid papaw. Plants flourish in moist woodland where there is plenty of leaf mold and they tolerate full or partial shade.

WILD FLOWERS TO GROW

There are seven small plants for dense shade, all are low and will enhance a small woodsy corner, but they vary in their requirements and not all are compatible.

An interesting ghostly plant is the Indian Pipe (*Monotropa uniflora*)—ghostly because it seeks the forest depths where the white waxen flowers stand out in the shadows. Each blossom is an inverted pipe with white flakes up the 6-inch stem. The plant blooms from June to August, and thrives in rich moist earth or in deciduous woods. Indian Pipes require acid soil. This plant has a wide range, flourishing from Japan to the Himalayas to New England! Transplanting it is a challenge because brittle roots clutch at the decaying matter around which they twine, and on which they feed. The best way to move it is to dig a large hole and take a good clump of earth including the compost to which the roots are attached. Support each clump in a deep box until you get it home. Dig an oversize hole and fill it in with soil from the forest. Set in the plant and keep it wet for a few days.

Pinesap or Beechdrops (*Monotropa hypopitys*) is similar to the Indian Pipe except for color, which varies from tawny brown to dark red. Also, this plant prospers in dry pine woods and acid soil where it flowers from July to September.

146

GREEN AND PINK AND WHITE

Pipsissewa (*Chimaphila umbellata*) and Striped Pipsissewa (*Chimaphila maculata*) are a joy for planting in deep woods. These low evergreen plants with roots that branch just under the ground litter have thick, dark green leaves, leathery and toothed, and with a dull gloss. They rise erect on 6-inch stems. Above the leaves, flowers reach up another 3 to 6 inches. These clusters of pinkish waxen blossoms appear in July and August. Pipsissewa needs acid soil and does well under pines or hemlocks. These plants are hardy, easy to transplant, and adapt readily to new environments. Both varieties thrive in the same habitat. The Striped Pipsissewa is so called for the light stripe down the center of each leaf.

The Wild Lily-of-the-Valley or Canada Mayflower (*Maianthemum canadense*) is another inhabitant of heavy shade. In spring, up comes a light green oval leaf; then rising above this, small, feathery white clusters of bloom. The leaf provides a green background for the miniature florets that otherwise might be missed. It thrives in acid soil. Roots do not stretch far, so plants are easy to move.

Anytime you are in the woods and discover the smooth shiny foliage of Wintergreen (*Gaultheria procumbens*), sometimes called Checkerberry, pause and break off a leaf to enjoy the pungent aroma. The evergreen leaves are

147

but 6 inches high; the bell-shaped flowers less than half an inch long hang on short stems under the leaves. Birds and field mice are attracted to the red berries that follow. This is a most adaptable woodland plant; thriving in clay, sand, humus, in wet or dry woods, and even in partial sunlight. It grows well in very acid soil as well as that with much less acidity.

Rattlesnake Plantain (*Epipactis tesselata*) is fine for a small area. A rosette of gray-green leaves spreads over the ground. Each leaf is attractively patterned with white lines. Plants grow in clusters and multiply by underground roots. This member of the orchid family, during the summer, sends up a stalk covered with very small white-fringed florets. Easy to transplant, it does best in acid soil and in proximity to rocks. Our plants thrive along the north side of a stone wall close to some boulders. Pine woods, oak, any place with rich deep, acid soil will suit. This fine plant is effective in terrariums where it grows all winter if planted in a little pocket of woods soil.

PARTRIDGEBERRY

One of the most delightful of all small plants for a shady woods area is the Partridgeberry or Twinberry (*Mitchella repens*). Trailing stems of round evergreen leaves the size of your little fingernail creep over the ground. From April to June pink, urn-shaped, fragrant flowers develop in pairs, followed in fall by bright red berries. Partridgeberry thrives in leaf mold, pine needles, or mossy areas, and must have acid soil. It grows under hemlocks, pines, or anywhere in deep woods. It is easy to transplant. Root the long running stems by covering them well with soil so that only the leaves are above ground. Partridgeberry is also invaluable for terrariums.

No longer need you cast a hopeless glance at those dark corners on your property where nothing has grown before. Each spot, large or small, can be converted into a choice woods garden or woodsy corner. Here in cool shade and in the atmosphere of a woodland, you will be tempted to linger and while away a minute or an hour. Here a variety of small flowers, leaf patterns, cushioned mosses, and trailing green will delight your eye while around you rises the scent of the woods.

FLOWERING PLANTS FOR DEEP SHADE

Blue Cohosh—*Caulophyllum thalictroides*

False Solomon's-Seal—*Smilacina racemosa*

Indian Pipe—*Monotropa uniflora*

Jack-in-the-Pulpit—*Arisaema triphyllum*

May Apple—*Podophyllum peltatum*

Partridgeberry—*Mitchella repens*

149

WILD FLOWERS TO GROW

Pinesap—*Monotropa hypopitys*

Pipsissewa—*Chimaphila umbellata*

Rattlesnake Plantain—*Epipactis tesselata*

Solomon's-Seal—*Polygonatum biflorum*

Striped Pipsissewa—*Chimaphila maculata*

Wild Ginger—*Asarum canadense*

Wild Lily-of-the-Valley—*Maianthemum canadense*

Wintergreen—*Gaultheria procumbens*

FERNS AND CLUB MOSSES
FOR DECIDUOUS WOODLAND

FERNS

Beech—*Dryopteris hexagonoptera*

Bracken—*Pteridium aquilinum*

Brittle—*Cystopteris fragilis*

Christmas—*Polystichum acrostichoides*

Cinnamon—*Osmunda cinnamomea*

Ebony Spleenwort—*Asplenium platyneuron*

Hay-Scented—*Dennstaedtia punctilobula*

Interrupted—*Osmunda claytoniana*

Leather or Wood Marginal—*Dryopteris marginalis*

Maidenhair—*Adiantum pedatum*

New York—*Aspidium noveboracenis*

Polypody—*Polypodium vulgare*

Rattlesnake—*Botrychium virginianum*

Royal—*Osmunda regalis*

Sensitive—*Onoclea sensibilis*

CLUB MOSSES

Ground Cedar—*Lycopodium complanatum*

Ground Pine—*obscurum*

Running Pine—*clavatum*

Shining Club Moss—*lucidulum*

A WILD GARDEN IN DEEP SHADE

FERNS AND MOSSES FOR HEMLOCK WOODS

FERNS

Beech—*Dryopteris hexagonoptera*
Bracken—*Pteridium aquilinum*
Brittle—*Cystopteris fragilis*
Christmas—*Polystichum acrostichoides*
Lady—*Athyrium filix-femina*
Leather or Wood Marginal—*Dryopteris marginalis*
Maidenhair—*Adiantum pedatum*
Oak—*Dryopteris linnaeana*
Ostrich—*Pteretis nodulosa*
Polypody—*Polypodium vulgare*
Rattlesnake—*Botrychium virginianum*

Silvery Spleenwort—*Athyrium thelypteroides*
Toothed or Common Wood—*Dryopteris spinulosa*

CLUB MOSSES

Ground Cedar—*Lycopodium complanatum*
Ground Pine—*obscurum*
Running Pine—*clavatum*
Shining Club Moss—*lucidulum*

9. For Streambanks and Boggy Places

You are fortunate indeed if you have a stream meandering or rushing through your place. The joys of a running brook are endless, and you can enhance them by designing a path that meanders close to and then away from the water. By clearing out undergrowth or weedy patches you will create space for wild flowers. Plan the plantings to provide surprises at turns and at natural stopping places, such as large rocks, along the path.

A streamside path can be 25 feet long—or 300 feet. The main thing is to assure full enjoyment of the stream. Along the banks of a stream—or creek or brook—are peaceful cool areas that breathe of remoteness and privacy. Sphagnum and other mosses cushion a weathered stump and rocks at the water's edge. A kingfisher hovers, dragonflies pause in mid air above still pools, and water beetles forever chase each other across the placid surface.

Along every brook there are native plants. And you can always introduce more. From the first spears of Skunk Cabbage in the spring on through the fall-blooming Turtleheads, many wildlings tempt you.

Everybody knows Skunk Cabbage (*Symplocarpus foetidus*)—that dramatic forerunner of spring—so common we forget how beautiful it is. The green-bronze-purple hood that shelters the true flower comes up through the muck, then opens into graceful curves.

Skunk Cabbage is found in acid to neutral soil and thrives along a shady streambank, and also in filtered sunlight. After a cold and snowy season, how we welcome the fresh spring green of these young leaves. When mature, they prove a pleasing contrast to the more delicate foliage of other woodland plants.

Indian Poke or American White hellebore (*Veratrum viride*) comes along with Skunk Cabbage, its light green leaves borne in tiers. Each one has many ribs and opens in crinkled parallel lines. The 3-foot plant is a joy all through early spring. The flowers, developing later, are unimportant; in early summer the plant disappears. Indian Poke is seldom on any conservation list, and people who have it are usually willing to share their plants. Move it in early spring. The root is poisonous to cattle and sheep.

THREE SMALL BEAUTIES

Certain wild flowers have a subtle beauty. For the streamside garden in spring, I propose three such small and delicate flowers whose appeal lies in their fragility. Each has some special delight, and all are easy to establish. The Wood Anemone (*Anemone quinquefolia*), often called Wind Flower, is named for the Greek wind god, *Anemos*. The small 1-inch, white-petaled flower on a 6-inch stem sways in every zephyr. The foliage, equally delicate, suggests the Maidenhair Fern.

Bellwort or Oakesia (*Uvularia sessilifolia*) is 8 inches high, and modestly hangs a 1-inch, yellow, bell-like bloom beneath slim, tapering, pale green leaves.

Goldthread (*Coptis trifolia*) is so named because of its bright yellow roots. These contributed to the store of medicinal herbs used in olden times by the country housewife. The small white flower rising on a 3- to 6-inch stem has golden anthers. Each is exquisite in its detail. Do take a look with a magnifying glass.

To make the most of these three flowers, buy and plant a minimum of a dozen each. Set them 2 inches apart in a small cleared area. One or two plants here and there would be lost.

Marsh Marigolds and Trout Lilies

Among the gayest flowers for the streambank are Marsh Marigolds or Cowslips (*Caltha palustris*). These sunny plants grow in shallow water as well as on nearby land.

In May they send up shiny butter-yellow flowers with feathery stamens and smooth heart-shaped leaves for background.

Adaptable Marsh Marigolds thrive in very acid, slightly acid, or neutral soil. They grow in sunny, wet meadows, or filtered shade, and reproduce readily by seed or by division. If you are going to move some from the wilds to your own brookside, you will need a pair of galoshes. Transplant in early spring—assuming, of course, that they are not on your local conservation list or that you are saving them from a building project. In either case, you may find yourself standing ankle-deep—or deeper— in swamp water and reaching down with bare hands into black mud. Gently separate the plants you want, and bring them home in a basket lined with wet newspaper. Plant at once.

On drier land nearby the Dog's-Tooth Violets (*Erythronium americanum*) are in bloom. These are sometimes called Trout Lilies, Yellow Adder's-Tongue, or Fawn Lilies. Each 2-inch blossom *is* like a Lily. In April and May in New England, the pointed, mottled, ribbonlike green foliage lies flat on last winter's dead leaves. You never seem to notice imminent flower stalks. One day there by the brook, you discover leaves, and in another day or so, you find dozens of golden flowers with curving reflexed petals—like a corps of ballet dancers. These biennials grow from bulblike roots, and need acid soil.

To establish Trout Lilies, clear a 2-foot-square area above a water line. In the center, set out a dozen mature bulbs, 2 inches apart and 2 inches deep. Until they become established, keep the area free of weeds. The foliage makes a fine ground cover in early summer. Later it disappears.

Spring Into Summer

Wild Lily-of-the-Valley (*Maianthemum canadense*) grows to 6 inches and each thin stem bears a few shiny pointed leaves, and in early spring, a tight plume of small white flowers. The plants spread so rapidly that they soon produce a quantity of blooms. Following the blossoms, beady red berries develop and persist until eaten by birds in the fall. Wild Lily-of-the-Valley thrives in humus-rich acid soil at the base of trees and stumps, above rocky outcroppings, as well as along the edge of paths. It is readily propagated from seeds and cuttings.

There are two easy-to-grow and attractive blue flowers for the streambank. The first is Forget-me-not (*Myosotis scorpioides*), blooming from May to July. Though a native of Europe and Asia, it grows wild in many parts of America. Small clusters of light blue flowers, each with a golden eye, make charming bouquets. The sprawling plant grows 6 to 12 inches high, and is often found partly in the water. It also lives on the banks above a stream, and there the foliage seems to emerge from the very stones.

The other blue flower is the Virginia Cowslip (*Mertensia virginica*). Native to the South, this flourishes as cheerfully along brooksides in the North. The nodding bell-like flowers are both blue and pink, but blue predominates. The plant grows to a foot or more and appears as Fern fronds uncurl in the spring. Our Virginia Cowslips grow in drifts among Royal Ferns. In summer, Cowslip foliage dies down, and the area is filled in with Fern. Another good companion is Wild Ginger whose leaves also cover the area from midsummer on. Transplant Virginia Cowslips immediately after they have flowered. They will colonize in woodland areas beneath deciduous trees. They require early spring sunshine.

WILD MINT AND WATERCRESS

Wild Mint (*Mentha arvensis*), that fresh green flavor in cool drinks, is also a fresh green fragrance at the water's edge. If you crush a leaf or brush against the foliage you are surrounded by a tangy pungence. Mint is a rich dark green plant, and in summer, furry white or lavender flowers form at the leaf joints.

157

Mint thrives almost anywhere, including the hot sunny vegetable garden. However, it seems most at home in filtered shade along a stream. It is good chopped into a sauce for lamb or cooked into jelly. And Mint makes a delightful tea. Pick fresh leaves, crush them slightly, and boil a few minutes. With honey and lemon juice, this is delicious. At the end of the season, hang up a few bunches to dry; the crumbled leaves may be used all winter.

Another pleasant streamside plant is Watercress (*Nasturtium officinale*). In spring, buy a bunch at the grocer's. Set it in a bowl of water. In a week or two the bowl will hold a mass of roots. Firmly anchor these rooted stems somewhere in the sandy stream bottom, preferably in a quiet little back-water with partial sun. All summer long you can enjoy Watercress sandwiches and salads, provided, of course, that you are sure of the purity of the stream. Blended, Watercress adds a wonderful spicy note to Vichyssoise. It also produces small, appealing white flowers.

Start Watercress as near the head of the brook as possible because it tends to travel with the current. Once planted, it will maintain itself for years. Not only you, but your neighbor downstream will find plantlets springing up along the water's edge, and in unexpected places.

FOR STREAMBANKS AND BOGGY PLACES

SUMMER INTO FALL

Toward the middle of summer, Jewelweed (*Impatiens biflora*) begins to bloom and it lasts through September with myriads of small brown-dotted orange flowers. Each blossom swings like a dainty jeweled earring on a slender stem. The rampant plant, with toothed green leaves and fleshy stems, grows 2 to 4 feet high, in any kind of soil. Ours burgeons on a rocky bank above the water and also partly in it. The leaves are reputed to be an antidote for poison ivy, when crushed and rubbed immediately on affected areas. In the fall the seed pods ripen. Touch one and it springs open tossing the seed several feet away.

SCARLET SPIRES

Along the banks of the brook in late summer blooms the vivid Cardinal Flower (*Lobelia cardinalis*). The plant grows 20 to 30 inches high and the blossoms come in long terminal clusters. The bright color makes a fiery glow even in shade. When the sun shines, it dazzles. How to tell a scarlet tanager from a Cardinal Flower? The brilliant birds often bathe in our stream near the red, red blossoms. Who's to say which is the brighter.

The first New England settlers sent the Cardinal

Flower back to England as an example of the floral wealth of the New World. This plant thrives with its feet in a moist streambank, but set it beyond the reach of running water lest it be pulled loose from the mooring roots. The flower has temperament as well as beauty. It reseeds and spreads readily but usually where *it* wants to grow and not always where I intend to establish it. Our plants turn up in different places every year or so.

To establish Cardinal Flowers successfully, clear a spot in filtered sunlight. Buy and set out young plants, and keep them free from weeds for a year or two. The Cardinal Flower will also bloom in drier areas, even in rock gardens and perennial borders.

Turtlehead (*Chelone glabra*) thrives in the full shade of deciduous trees and also in partial sun. The plant grows to 3 feet. Slim pointed leaves develop opposite each other all the way up the stalk. At the top is a cluster of flowers, either white touched with pink or all deep pink. These come in late summer and continue until frost. Each floret is about an inch long, two-lipped, and somewhat turtle-shaped. Watch a bee enter and observe how the lower lip moves with his weight so that the blossom seems to be chewing up the bee.

Violets prosper on a shady streambank, in a sunny meadow, in boggy or high dry areas. Violets are among the most amiable of plants and grow just about anywhere. The nature of the soil seems unimportant, acid or alkaline, heavy or light.

Wild Iris

Every sunny wet meadow and swampy place is a prospective area for growing the Large Blue Flag (*Iris versicolor*). Lance-shaped leaves first appear in April, but it is June before you see the 4-inch flower: blue-violet touched with yellow. The whole plant stands 2 to 3 feet high. Though each flower blooms briefly, others keep coming for many days. During two or three weeks every June these blossoms transform a meadow into an Oriental scene! The plant is tough and hardy, flourishing in boggy areas; it can take wet feet practically the year around. To bloom properly, it must have sun. This Iris, which is not particular about soil, may be transplanted at any time and it increases rapidly. The Iris rootstock is called a rhizome; always be sure there is at least one leaf-fan to each piece of rhizome when you separate for transplanting.

The blue Crested Dwarf Iris (*Iris cristata*) that grows wild all through the mountains of North Carolina, also thrives in semishaded areas of our New England meadows. It will grow in slightly damp as well as drier spots.

Though Water Hemlock (*Cicuta maculata*) is related to the Hemlock that poisoned Socrates, it is quite safe to raise. The branching plant grows 2 to 5 feet high. Flat clusters of white flowers rising above the leaves suggest Queen Anne's Lace. Each tiny floret is furry and delightful, especially under a magnifying glass.

In Wet Meadows

In your sunny wet meadow, set out a few plants of the 3-foot-high Swamp Rose Mallow (*Hibiscus moscheutos*). This flower from Europe has naturalized here and blooms in early summer. The bright pink blossoms, 4 to 6 inches across, smell somewhat of musk. Several blooms look lovely floating in a large flat silver bowl, or other container. The plants are not fussy about soil, although they do best if it is nearly neutral. The foliage is slow to appear in spring. After a few years, when the clumps have increased in size, they may be divided. These hardy perennials bloom regularly.

Golden Alexander (*Zizia aurea*), sometimes called Meadow Parsnip, is like a soft yellow and smaller version of Queen Anne's lace. It spreads freely through low, marshy places, and from a distance looks like a golden mist.

Tall Meadow Rue (*Thalictrum polygamum*) is a

162

graceful 3- to 6-foot perennial. In spring when you first see the foliage you may think it is Columbine, so similar are the leaves and of the same blue-green. This easy-to-grow plant thrives in moist or dry locations and brings great charm to the field. It blooms in early summer and is covered for weeks with branching clusters of white flowers. Each soft and downy floret is like a diminutive Dandelion.

Joe-Pye Weed or Perennial Ageratum (*Eupatorium purpurem*), 3 to 5 feet high, grows in sunny and semi-shaded swamps, and also in drier spots. The florets are miniscule and crowded into a cluster at the top of the plant. The pinkish-purple flowers are outstanding in August. Near us in Connecticut there is a house painted exactly the same color. I never would have dreamed the shade would be as lovely on clapboards as in a meadow, but it is. What completes the effectiveness of the whole scene is that the house is set in a small lawn surrounded by a wild area of Joe-Pye Weed.

The Wild Calla (*Calla palustris*), often called Water Arum, is a delightful miniature a foot high, and blooming in early summer. The leaves are heart-shaped and the snowy flower has a rolling rim. This Calla grows in sunny, boggy areas where the water is only a few inches deep. It looks like a small edition of the large Callas that flood

Mexican flower markets at Christmastime, and our own flower shops in spring.

The Wild Calla needs acid soil. The creeping rootstock wanders through the mud and thus the plant spreads. The flowers are followed by clusters of red berries, rather like those of Jack-in-the-Pulpit. If you sow the seeds as soon as they are ripe in flats of mud and set these at the edge of a brook or in a marshy spot, seedlings will appear and a year later you can put the plantlets in permanent positions.

THE GENTIANS

An interesting blue meadow flower of late summer is the Bottle Gentian (*Gentiana andrewsi*), the same color as the Fringed Gentian but a little earlier to bloom. Several blossoms are clustered on an erect 1- to 2-foot stem. They look like buds waiting to open. But of course they never "open," although they aren't as "closed" as they appear. The bees find a way to enter. Propagation is by division of the clumps in spring. The plant adapts to many soils but does best in a slightly damp place.

The Fringed Gentian (*G. crinita*) is the best-known Gentian of all, and a most temperamental plant. It starts to bloom at the end of the summer and remains in flower for many weeks. It grows in candelabra form, the plant 1 to 2 feet tall. It may have a single flower or several dozen, all deep, dark blue with beautifully fringed petals. It thrives on grassy hillsides where it is moist and sunny, in semishade, or on a hummock of grass in a swamp. This Gentian is biennial, another reason why it seems to be temperamental. It is also a favorite food of deer which may explain an occasional sudden disappearance.

Fringed Gentians may be naturalized in moist low pastures. Collect the seed and scatter it right through the meadow where tufts of grass are thinnest or where you have first stripped off areas of sod. Since Fringed Gentian is on conservation lists in many states, seed sowing is an excellent way to start it on your own land. Keep gathering the seed annually. You can never have too many of these shaggy-petaled flowers that in their deep tones reflect the blue of autumn skies.

PLANTS FOR THE BROOKSIDE

White, Variable and Off-White, Green Tints

Bloodroot—*Sanguinaria canadensis*
Bunchberry—*Cornus canadensis*
Buttonbush—*Cephalanthus occidentalis*
Culver's Root—*Veronicastrum virginicum*
Dutchman's-Breeches—*Dicentra cucullaria*
False Solomon's-Seal—*Smilacina racemosa*
Foamflower—*Tiarella cordifolia*

WILD FLOWERS TO GROW

Goldthread—*Coptis trifolia*
Groundnut—*Panax trifolium*
Indian Poke—*Veratrum viride*
Large Flowering Trillium—
Trillium grandiflorum
Lizard's-Tail—*Saururus cernuus*
May Apple—*Podophyllum peltatum*
Partridgeberry—*Mitchella repens*
Pipsissewa—*Chimaphila Umbellata*
Star Flower—*Trientalis borealis*

Sweet-scented Bedstraw—
Galium triflorum
Sweet White Violet—*Viola blanda*
Toothwort—*Dentaria diphylla*
Turtlehead—*Chelone glabra*
Wild Lily-of-the-Valley—
Maianthemum canadense
Wild Mint—*Mentha arvensis*
Wood Anemone—*Anemone quinquefolia*
Wood Sorrel—*Oxalis acetosella*

Clear Blue, Lavender, and Purple

American Brooklime—*Veronica americana*
Common Violet—*Viola cucullata*
Crested Dwarf Iris—*Iris cristata*
False Dragonhead—*Physostegia virginiana*
Forget-me-not—*Myosotis scorpioides*
Heartleaf Twayblade—*Listera cordata*
Jack-in-the-Pulpit—*Arisaema triphyllum*

Skunk Cabbage—*Symplocarpus foetidus*
Spiderwort—*Tradescantia virginiana*
Virginia Cowslip—*Mertensia virginica*
Wild Blue Phlox—*Phlox divaricata*
Wild Geranium—*Geranium maculatum*

Yellow, Orange-Yellow, and Orange

Bellwort—*Uvularia sessilifolia*
Blue Cohosh—*Caulophyllum thalictroides*

Canada Lily—*Lilium canadense*
Dog's-Tooth Violet—*Erythronium americanum*

FOR STREAMBANKS AND BOGGY PLACES

Jewelweed—*Impatiens biflora*

Lady's-Slipper—*Cypripedium parviflorum*

Marsh Marigold—*Caltha palustris*

Pink, Purple-Red, and Red

Joe-Pye Weed—*Eupatorium purpureum*

Moccasin Flower—*Cypripedium acaule*

Oswego Tea—*Monarda didyma*

Showy Orchis—*Orchis spectabilis*

Spring Beauty—*Claytonia virginica*

Wake-Robin—*Trillium erectum*

SOME FLOWERS FOR MOIST AND BOGGY AREAS

Blue Flag—*Iris versicolor*

Bottle Gentian—*Gentiana andrewsi*

Canada Lily—*Lilium canadense*

Crested Dwarf Iris—*Iris cristata*

Day Lily—*Hemerocallis fulva*

Fringed Gentian—*Gentiana crinita*

Golden Alexanders—*Zizia aurea*

Joe-Pye Weed—*Eupatorium purpureum*

Swamp Rose Mallow—*Hibiscus moscheutos*

Tall Meadow Rue—*Thalictrum polygamum*

Turk's-Cap Lily—*Lilum superbum*

Violet-*Viola* (except Bird's-foot—*Viola pedata*)

Water Hemlock—*Cicuta maculata*

Wild Calla—*Calla palustris*

10. Summer Flowers
for a Sunny Meadow

While spring is the time for woodland wild flowers, summer is the time in the meadow. From early summer till frost, wild flowers dominate open sunny meadows.

A meadow is a joy. In early morning fresh cool grasses sparkle with dew, dew that brings out the wet growing scent of a summer day at its start, dew that hangs heavy on the shaggy golden Hawkweed of June and the prim Butterfly Weed of August. A meadow has fragrance in the early morning and all day long, but the perfume is heaviest in the rain and on warm nights.

A meadow is full of activity. Birds nest in the feathery grass; the praying mantis stalks his prey; insects go about their work. When the sun sets, a summer meadow comes ablaze with hosts of fireflies. Here is a place where we "see" the wind for flowers and grasses catch it in ripples and toss it back and forth.

168

SUMMER FLOWERS FOR A SUNNY MEADOW

LARGE OR SMALL

A meadow may be one acre or ten; a meadow also may
be a sunny stretch along the wilderness edge of your
place. It can be a section of lawn that you stop mowing
and plant with wild flowers. Instead of so much neatly-
cropped green you could let nature have her way with a
part of it, and give her a helping hand. With a few wild
plants to start and the seed of a number more, you can
create your own meadow. A meadow, to be a proper one,
must have sunlight. Aside from sun, whether it is high
or low, wet or dry, rocky or composed of deep loam,
there are flowers for every situation.

If you have a field, some flowers and grasses are already
there, especially if you have held off mowing until midsummer or later. What a pleasure to add a few more
plants. To get a new variety started, you could just broadcast your gathered seed, but it would be surer if you dug
out the sod first. You can also sow the seed in a separate
bed and transplant one year later, as suggested in Chapter
4.

Once you have established a meadow, care and upkeep
are negligible. It is important, however, not to mow before mid-August, and some meadows are best mowed only

every third year. This permits plants to reseed and multiply.

Here are some of the delightful summer and fall wild flowers that make our own meadow such a delight.

In June, Hawkweed transforms the south meadow into a sea of flowing gold. These are the flowers that play with the wind as it ripples through their yellow-fringed blooms. Hawkweed (*Hieracium canadense*), sometimes called Devil's-Paintbrush, grows by the thousands in open, sunny, well-drained land. Plants thrive in gritty, rocky areas where the soil is dreadfully poor. Each furry-leaved plant lies on the ground, a rosette of green. From its center a flower stalk rises—a stalk 8 to 12 inches high. The clustered heads of gold or orange flowers, like small Dandelions, last a full month, coming and going. These are not for bouquets: once picked they soon wilt.

The downy wisps of seed may be gathered in July. If broadcast, they come up where field grass isn't growing too thick, but it is best to sow them where you have first bared a strip of earth.

DAISY TYPES

Following Hawkweed, come the well-loved, golden Black-eyed Susan (*Rudbeckia hirta*) that thrives in rich grassy meadows. But Black-eyed Susans also live where soil is poor. In such a place, if you scatter a little fertilizer around the plants, the following year they double in size and produce twice as many blooms. Black-eyed Susans begin to flower late in June and continue into August. They are easy to transplant and easy to naturalize.

Some varieties are biennial. Many are perennial, and I have noticed specific clumps returning each year. You may readily start them from seed, but we have also moved mature plants with good results. They make fine cut flowers, lasting nearly a week indoors. This is a wild flower that you can pick successfully *and* legally. It is a native to the United States; the plant is reputed to have originally traveled eastward from Colorado in bales of hay, and by the same means crossed the ocean to Europe.

Along with the Black-eyed Susans comes the Common White Daisy (*Chrysanthemum leucanthemum*), the flower of graduation daisy chains and of he-loves-me, he-loves-me-not: a flower praised in poem and song. I once attended a garden wedding where the bride carried a bouquet of Daisies. It was as beautiful as any I've seen—both wedding and bouquet. This Daisy is for everyone and for every kind of sunny location. Plants grow beautifully with Black-eyed Susans outdoors, and combine equally well in indoor arrangements.

WILD FLOWERS TO GROW

BETONY AND BUTTERFLY WEED

Wood Betony (*Pedicularis canadensis*) is sometimes called by the odd name of Lousewort. Years ago farmers believed that when the sheep ate it, it transferred an insect to the animals that settled on their skin—hence the name. This was proved false, and I think the plant well deserves the prettier title of Wood Betony. Each short feathery leaf is like a green ladder. The 8-inch-tall flowers have a carefree, windblown look, somewhat like a disheveled rosette. Blooms are red or yellow or a mingling of both. Try a cluster in a small blue china or copper vase for a bedside bouquet.

Butterfly Weed (*Asclepias tuberosa*) is one of the most attractive members of the Milkweed Family. Because of its thick tuberous root that penetrates deep into the earth, it thrives in hard, dry, packed soil. The orange flowers open in flat clusters and are so vivid they catch the eye at a great distance. It also attracts a number of butterflies. You can do a lot worse than go out some sunny morning and sit on a cushion in your meadow and watch the bees and butterflies hovering over this flower. The blossoms are followed by beaklike pods that make fine additions to dried arrangements. The pods are attractive

172

both before they open and after they have tossed away their shiny silken seeds.

Butterfly Weed grows from 1 to 2 feet, thrives in gravelly soil, and the same plant comes up year after year. Because of the long root it is difficult to transplant, but get all the root and the plant will readily adjust to any soil. Even better, select small specimens. For best results and winter survival, give full sun and good drainage. Seeds sown in the fall produce plants that may flower at the end of the next summer. Butterfly Weed can easily be propagated from root cuttings. Take several 1- to 2-inch root cuttings in May, set them below the surface of sandy soil, and keep slightly moist. Soon they will sprout into new plants.

Carrot and Yucca

Queen Anne's Lace (*Daucus carota*) is a member of the Parsley Family. The lacy geometric design of the blooms and their perfection of detail as well as the feathery blossoms themselves make this a most desirable wild flower. All summer in drifts of white they sweep over the landscape. When the flower passes, it browns and curls up into something like a bird's nest. The plant grows in dry soil everywhere. In Switzerland, due no doubt to the fine

Alpine air, flower heads are immense. From a distance, you would think the mountain meadow where they blossom a field of snow. This is probably one of the plants that has come to us from Europe.

Queen Anne's Lace is magnificent in a bouquet. Indoors you have an even better opportunity to observe it closely. The blossom is composed of a radiating pattern of small florets. In the center, you frequently discover a single, small, deep purple one. The foliage *is* highly scented by an aromatic oil. Perhaps it is this strong odor that attracts butterflies, bees, moths, and other insects.

Yucca (*Hespero-Yucca whipplei*), a large and ferocious perennial, looks more at home on a Mexican mountainside than in a New England meadow. Actually Yucca is a relative of the Joshua Tree of the Mojave Desert, and there are many species. Adam's Needle (*Y. filamentosa*) does well in the East. All like hot sunny, dry spots where soil is gritty and poor. The Yucca plant consists of a huge rosette of sword-shaped leaves, sharp at the tip, with occasional white threads trailing from the spines. A 6-foot flower stalk rises from the center of the leaves. Toward the top a cluster of waxen white blooms unfolds.

Each parent plant produces children nearby; these are miniature rosettes, less dangerous and more manageable, and hence the ones to transplant. The best time is early in spring; they soon grow to great clumps like the parent. If you have ever seen these flowers towering in the canyons of the California coast, pure white against blue sky and tall redwoods, you will appreciate their drama and be delighted to know that there are Yuccas that will flourish, small-scale, for you.

MARVELOUS LILIES

Four of the meadow Lilies are irresistible. The Canada Lily (*Lilium canadense*) grows to 5 feet and blooms in June and July. The stalk is encircled by tiers of foliage, every tier consisting of six pointed, lancelike leaves. Several golden flowers spring up from the apex of the plant, each nodding on its slender stem. A blossom is about 3 inches long, yellow or orange, and spotted brown inside. There is color variation from plant to plant. On sunny days the Canada Lily, like the Butterfly Weed, is surrounded by bees and butterflies. The drooping flower cup protects the nectar from rain.

These Lilies grow in moist, sunny meadows in fertile loam. They flourish in part shade or full sun. The soil may be damp, but they must have good drainage; they won't live in a stagnant bog. Set the bulbs 4 to 5 inches deep, and they will multiply rapidly. Most Lilies have the habit of working their way down; if they are not planted

175

deep enough, they tend to solve the difficulty by themselves. However, they cannot push themselves up, so it is better to plant too shallow than too deep.

The Day Lily (*Hemerocallis fulva*) runs rampant and sweeps through New England meadows as well as along its roadsides. Here it flowers in July and August. It grows 2 to 5 feet high, and while the flowers last only a day more keep coming. A single stalk may produce eight or nine red-gold blossoms, and two or three may be open at one time. The ribbonlike foliage grows so dense that it crowds out other plants in the area, including weeds. Day Lilies are tough, hardy, easy to move, and best transplanted or divided in spring before the large leaves get in your way. Slice down into a clump of roots and let each division have a good piece of green foliage at the top. Plants rapidly take hold and thrive in a new location.

The petals of the Turk's Cap Lily (*Lilium superbum*) are so reflexed that the flower shape suggests a Turkish cap. The color, a flaming orange, varies slightly, paling or deepening, from plant to plant. It needs rich acid soil, with lots of humus. Give this Lily good drainage. It will grow where there is plenty of moisture and also where it is hot and dry. It thrives in full sun or partial shade. Its flowering season follows that of the Canada Lily.

The Wood Lily (*Lilium philadelphicum*) does not

176

droop, but raises up its orange-scarlet petals, tulip-style. The flower appears at the top of a stem that may be as high as 3 feet. It opens in June and July, grows in partial shade or full sun, needs acid soil and lots of organic matter. It will also thrive in hot, sandy, dry earth far from moisture. The color is bright as a flaming torch.

FLOWERS FOR SUNNY MEADOWS

Black-eyed Susan—*Rudbeckia hirta*
Butterfly Weed—*Asclepias tuberosa*
Devil's-Paintbrush—*Hieracium canadense*
Oxeye-Daisy—*Chrysanthemum leucanthemum*
Queen Anne's Lace—*Daucus carota*
Wood Betony—*Pedicularis canadensis*
Yucca-Hespero—*Yucca whipplei*

11. Native Plants for Food and Fun

Our ingenious ancestors knew how to make Elderberries into ink and Irish Moss into blanc-mange. They washed their clothes in soap made from Bouncing Bet, and they got honey by stupifying bees with the brown, dustlike spores of Puffballs. They read by the light of homemade Bayberry candles and slept on mattresses of fragrant Bedstraw.

In the woods they could prepare a meal from Milkweed or Day Lilies, and quench their thirst with the juice of Wild Grapes. If they got poison ivy, they rubbed it with a crushed Jewelweed leaf. A paste of Solomon's-Seal leaves was applied to bruises, and according to Girarde's *Herbal*, this removed "any black and blue spots gotten by women's willfulneess in stumbling on their hastie husbands' fists."

You may not wish to do your laundry with the suds of Bouncing Bet or write with Elderberry ink, and your husband may not have a "hastie fist," but Bayberry candle-making is still fun, Elderberries in griddle cakes are delicious, and Milkweed shoots and Day Lily buds add zest to a modern meal. Food grown by the hand of man is not our only source of nourishment. Everywhere nature is generously willing to provide delicious things to eat.

Native plants usually are of stronger flavor than the familiar vegetables and fruits. To enjoy them, you need an adventurous attitude. As with olives, you may not relish the first bite, but if you persist, you will discover a world of new tastes. But be sure you have the right plant before you eat it. While many native plants are edible, a few are poisonous, as all parts of Datura or Jimson-Weed, certain mushrooms, the berries of white (not red) Sumac, and the roots and leaves of Indian Poke. And if you are planning on Watercress sandwiches, first make sure of the purity of the water in which it is growing.

Today when we eat nature's bounty, we are rediscovering old customs. As long ago as 200 B.C., Cato recommended Wild Asparagus, and it was a favorite food of the Emperor Augustus later. Of comparable flavor and equally delectable are Milkweed shoots. To prepare these, pour boiling water over them and boil for one minute to remove bitterness. Chickweed can be stewed into a nourishing and delicious dish like spinach. Young sprouts of Bladder Campion, simmered until tender, then salted and buttered, taste somewhat like green peas. In Minorca, nearly a century ago, locusts destroyed the crops, but the

179

Islanders survived, largely because of the prevalence of Bladder Campion.

An oldtime dependable favorite in Europe is the root of the Evening Primrose. Boiled, the roots are not only nutritious but good: rather like a potato but sweeter. In spring, uncurling Fern fronds bring a rich earthy flavor to the table. These hold their color when cooked briefly, then buttered. The Ostrich Fern, the Common Brake, and the Royal Fern are especially flavorful.

Memorable Menus

Some years ago in Guatemala, I recall how strange it seemed to be eating cooked flowers for dinner, and how good they were. In New England, Day Lilies are equally delicious. Gather the buds when they are large but unopened, or just opening. Boil a few minutes, then butter and salt them as you do peas. These are relished by Orientals, and you will easily see why. Milkweed blossoms, harvested when about to open, are also delectable. They are like broccoli but with a distinctive flavor of their own. Boil in several waters.

Then there is Wild Mustard. Gather when in bud or just opening. Pour boiling water over the flowers, let stand half a minute, drain, cover with fresh boiling water, boil three minutes, season with salt and butter, and serve.

(Many of these wild-food suggestions are from that fine book, *Stalking the Wild Asparagus,* by Euell Gibbons, published by the David McKay Company, 1962.)

The versatile Watercress has many uses, some familiar, some new. Just be sure it is growing in pure water. Chopped and blended into cottage cheese, it enhances salads. In various parts of the country, Watercress grows wild. I have discovered it in the coastal redwood canyons of California where, like all things in that fabulous state, it is twice as big as our eastern variety. In fact, it is so prolific there that you are tempted to take home a basketful and use it like spinach. For pure ambrosia, do just this, and cook but briefly.

Watercress also makes delicious soup. Prepare a cream-soup base with two tablespoons of butter, one tablespoon chopped onions or chives, one and one-half tablespoons flour, one quarter teaspoon salt, pepper to taste, and two cups of milk. Pack a measuring cup with fine-chopped Watercress. Blend this into the piping hot, but never boiling, cream-soup base. Decorate wtih sprigs of Watercress, Parsley, or both.

SALAD GREENS

For tang in a salad, mix in a few Dandelion leaves that are small and spring-tender. To remove bitterness, soak in salt water for several hours first, then dry, and use. Young leaves of the Common Violet also bring a new flavor to a bowl of tossed greens. The foliage of the Blue Chicory that opens feathery blossoms in summer meadows is delightful combined with the Lettuces, Violets, and Dandelions.

If you cannot find enough Wild Asparagus to cook for a meal, chop a few spears into the salad. Wild Onions taste somewhat different from those in cultivation and also are desirable. Chickweed in the flower bed may enrage you, but in salad you will love it. A few Mint leaves bring welcome freshness to other greens.

Mint is popular for many drinks. Mint tea is a favorite of mine. This tea with honey and homemade bread beside a January hearthfire is hard to beat. In Switzerland, I learned about making Mint Tea with fresh-picked leaves steeped in boiling water until they darken to the desired strength. It was an old custom to rub down the dinner table with Mint leaves before a meal. Stimulating to the appetite, I was told.

BERRIES AND LEAVES

Whenever I visit a Polish friend, I enjoy a cup of tea made from dried Raspberries. This delicious beverage sweetened with honey seems the distillation of June. My friend tells me that in Poland the leaves are also dried and made into tea. Not only is this highly flavorful, but it is a country custom to give a cup or two a day of this Raspberry tea to a woman near the end of pregnancy to ease her delivery.

Dried blossoms of Red Clover make a meadow-fragrant drink. To make a Wintergreen tea, pour boiling water over fresh-cut-up leaves, let stand over low heat until it darkens to your taste. Adding honey and lemon juice brings out the flavor. Sassafras tea is another of my favorites. Make it from the roots of saplings which you can easily identify by the mitten-shaped leaves. Scrub the roots, cut up and boil them until the water turns red. You may use the same roots several times.

In late winter, try fresh Maple sap, which has been boiled a half hour or so, instead of water for any kind of tea. A beverage made with Maple sap is both delicious and healthful.

Wilderness areas are laden with raw materials for jam and jelly. How often I have wandered through Cape Cod meadows in July gathering wild Blackberries. Few Blackberries excel those grown near salt water. In New Hampshire and Vermont, we have picked wild Raspberries by the bucketful. And near us in Connecticut a vast field of

Blueberries offers its fruit. Over much of the country, wild Grapes are available. All these make fine jams.

Along the Atlantic coast, Beach Plums provide ripened fruit for jelly. Hips from the Rugosa Rose are also good for a jam, that helps supply your winter need for vitamin C. Wild Strawberries make wonderful jam. But for me this is well-nigh impossible. When they ripen in our meadow, I cannot resist eating as I pick, and I am lucky if I have the strength of character to gather into my basket enough for two for breakfast.

Violet-blossom sandwiches are amusing, a gay note for luncheon. How delicious are thin slices of white bread with purple blossoms in between. Rose-petal sandwiches, made with herb butter, are also pleasant, and you might surprise overnight guests with rose petals cut up in scrambled eggs. (First trim off the bitter base of each.) Candied Wild Ginger root rivals candied orange and grapefruit peel in flavor and is made the same way.

Wild Grape leaves (also those from cultivated Grapes), when picked young, are delightful rolled around chopped meat and baked or boiled until tender.

MOTH PROTECTION

Native plants, aside from their possibilities as food, have other uses that contribute to the pleasure and convenience of today's living. No need to line your closet with Cedar wood to discourage moths; a bag of Red Cedar chips gives equal protection. Dried chopped sphagnum moss provides an excellent medium for sprouting seeds.

Scotch Broom makes attractive hearth brushes. Gather and bind branches together with a stout cord, and you've a gay green whisk for putting fireplace ashes where they belong. Children enjoy weaving these fibrous twigs into baskets.

Some autumn, experiment with Bayberry candles. It takes a lot of berries for even a candle or two, but it is worthwhile for the fragrance while burning. The pungent Bayberry scent seems almost faint in the candles you buy; perhaps manufacturers dilute the wax. To make the candles, boil the berries and let the wax that rises to the surface harden. Remove this and remelt. Dip a wick up and down in it to make a candle as fat as you want.

For Children

Children love to play with native plant materials. A Milkweed seed pod makes a boat, or a cradle for a doll who may be covered with a blanket of Mullein leaf. Pine needles tied in bunches make tiny people. Trim their skirts evenly, stand them on a table, and blow them across it in a race.

WILD FLOWERS TO GROW

Children create wonderful shapes by sticking Burdock burrs together. Dandelion stems, split and rolled back, form curly-haired dolls. As a child, I used to play with these by the hour. Then I would blow three times on the downy white globe of a Dandelion gone to seed. The remaining wisps told me the hour.

Whatever your age, remember to suck nectar from the base of Wild Honeysuckle blossoms in June or the heart of a Sweet Clover bloom on a midsummer day. And chew Spruce Gum which tastes of woods and evergreens. Make pink lemonade by mashing red, never the poisonous white, Sumac berries; simmer and strain them, adding honey and ice.

Many of us respond warmly to the thought of living off the land. Today we can perhaps do this only briefly on a camping trip, but we can use natural foods much more than we do.

What we bring home from the wilds to eat or use is invariably satisfying and fun, and so is the gathering. Wander at dawn or dusk, or on a sunny afternoon through woods and meadows and along streams with a basket in hand. You will be looking, smelling, discovering, clipping here, and snipping there. What a wonderful way to spend a few hours.

We are missing something if we don't take a page from

the past and introduce some of this food and fun into our family lives.

WILD PLANTS FOR FOOD AND FLAVOR

Beach Plums—*Prunus maritima*
Blackberries—*Rubus flagellaris*
Bladder Campion—*Silene latifolia*
Blueberries—*Vaccinium* sp.
Chicory—*Cichorium intybus*
Chickweed—*Stellaria media*
Common Brake—*Pteris aquilinum*
Common Violet—*Viola cucullata*
Dandelion—*Taraxacum officinale*
Day Lily—*Hemerocallis fulva*
Elderberries—*Sambucus canadensis*
Evening Primrose—*Oenothera biennis*
Honeysuckle—*Lonicera japonica*
Huckleberry—*Gaulussacia* sp.
Irish Moss—*Chondrus crispus*
Milkweed—*Asclepias syriaca*
Ostrich Fern—*Pteretis pennsylvanica*

Puffballs—*Lycoperdon bovista*
Raspberries—*Rubus strigosus*
Red Clover—*Trifolium pratense*
Royal Fern—*Osmunda regalis*
Sassafras—*Sassafras albidum*
Spruce Gum—*Picea* sp.
Watercress—*Nasturtium officinale*
Wild Asparagus—*Asparagus officinalis*
Wild Garlic—*Allium canadense*
Wild Ginger—*Asarum canadense*
Wild Grapes—*Vitis* sp.
Wild Mint—*Mentha piperita*
Wild Mustard—*Barbarea vulgaris*
Wild Rose—*Rosa rugosa*
Wild Strawberries—*Fragaria virginiana*
Wintergreen—*Gaultheria procumbens*

12. Small World Under Glass

A wonderful way to enjoy wild flowers and woods plants indoors is to grow them in a terrarium. Once you learn about the terrarium method, no glass container in your house will be safe. You can create diminutive woodland scenes in anything from a drinking glass to a fish bowl.

A terrarium is a lovely green world under glass, a miniature woodland where the eye can wander and the imagination roam. Here stands a hill, a meadow, a canyon perhaps, all Lilliputian. With a few minutes of care every week, this glass-enclosed landscape will give you pleasure for months.

The first terrarium was made in England by Dr. Nathaniel Ward. A butterfly collector, he one day brought a rare chrysalis indoors to watch it hatch. For protection, he set it in a covered glass jar. With the chrysalis came a chunk of soil. Immediately the earth began to sprout, and long after the butterfly had flown away, Dr. Ward had a garden of lovely small plants under glass. Soon others followed his example, and the containers for these gardens under glass became known as Wardian cases.

The woods is the place to go for material, though if there are no woods near you, you can purchase appropriate plants in greenhouses or buy them through wild flower catalogues. Going to the woods is of course the most fun. Fall is the ideal time. Check the conservation list for your state, but happily many of the things effective in terrariums are unlikely to be on it.

Have you a fish bowl, a brandy snifter, or an aquarium large or small? Even a glass teakettle will do. Tumblers of clear glass make delightful miniature enclosed gardens. Bowls and containers for terrariums may also be purchased in variety stores and florist shops. You need a cover for each one. Plexiglass, and unbreakable, cut to fit, is good. Standard glass will do too, and the hardware clerk will cut it and file the edges smooth. You also need a pair of long-handled tweezers from a second-hand medical-supply house (with these you can plant a long-necked bottle or carafe), a bulb sprayer from the five-and-ten, and scissors—that's all.

GATHERING TIME

Materials can be found in woodland, meadows, and at the roadside any time right up to Christmas, or until the ground is frozen or covered with snow. Gather very small Ferns (keeping everything in scale), some 1 inch high, a few 2, 3, and 4 inches, none taller unless you are working with a large, deep aquarium. Search in dry fields where birches grow for 1-inch Lichens, Pink Earth Lichen, Goblet Lichen, and that wonderful red-tipped variety called British Soldiers. If you examine this one under a magnifying glass, you'll find the red parts look like clusters of red apples at the top of a stalk. Enlarged it is astounding.

You'll want Mosses, sphagnum and a variety of others, some with long "fur" and some with short, some flexible and some stiff. Find, if you can, the shell-like fungus that grows on dead trees, and pieces of interesting bark. Bring in lengths of vines, Reindeer Moss, that tangle of gray featheriness that stiffens when dry and goes limp as a sponge when wet. Anything small and alive that attracts you is a possibility for use in your terrarium.

In spite of frosts, many Ferns appear untouched. Among the best of the taller kinds for terrariums are Ebony Spleenwort (*Asplenium platyneuron*) which grows along roads, and the Rock Fern (*Polypodium vulgare*), spreading like a blanket on huge boulders in damp or dry woods. Among the wild flowers suitable for terrarium use are Wintergreen (*Gaultheria procumbens*) with rich, shiny leaves and bright red berries to give a holiday air, and Pipsissewa (*Chimaphila umbellata*), which produces a pair of white-striped, stiff saw-edged leaves on a reddish stem. The Rattlesnake Plantain (*Epipactis repens*) is loveliest of all. We never tire of studying at close range the infinitely varied leaf markings.

In addition to wild flowers and Ferns, you will want a few trowelsful of leaf mold. With materials and equipment in hand you are ready to plant. Spread newspapers on floor or table and place a good lamp above you.

Wash and polish the glass containers till they sparkle. Those made of clear glass are best, glass that "wiggles" obscures a planting. Suppose you start with a large brandy snifter. First line the bottom with soft moss. Put it in upside-down so only the green surface shows through, and no earth is visible. Keep the horizon line of the scene you are creating below the widest part of the container; avoid getting a "high-waisted" look by setting the material up too far. Keep the whole scene well below the middle line.

STEP-BY-STEP PREPARATION

On top of the moss, spread a thin layer of leaf mold. In this you will plant the Ferns. Next, select a piece of substantial short-haired moss, flat and stiff, and make a bank of it up one side. Work in leaf mold behind the moss to hold it on its side to form a steep hill. On top of the hill, plant your tallest Fern, choosing one with three to five fronds. To plant, roll up each Fern root and wrap it in leaf mold. The unfolding fronds will then bend grace- fully creating pleasant curves. Dribble a few 1-inch Ferns down the sides of the hill at the edge next to the glass. Leave the center of the moss hill smooth and open. Your small landscape is now on two levels, a hill and a flat low part.

Opposite the hill, create a rolling rise and plant there a Pipsissewa, Rattlesnake Plantain, or a tiny evergreen tree, keeping a low path through the middle of the terrarium between the rise and the hill. A terrarium with a path is more interesting. Now perhaps you have a 2-inch hill on the right with tall Ferns, a 1-inch rise on the left with different lower growth, all on upside-down moss. You may have a path between these opposites, a sort of low valley providing a passage through. On the floor of the valley, shape and lay flat, short-haired moss. With tweezers insert tiny Ferns, Lichens, and bits of moss where different levels and mosses join. This way you conceal leaf mold and roots and the workings of your design.

Now your picture comes to life. You do not want clutter. Keep it simple and let each appealing treasure stand out where it can be appreciated. There are many ways of designing a terrarium planting. Try different ones, create your own plan, and don't follow anyone else's in detail because the charm for you will lie in the composition that you evolve.

Here are some guides:

(1) Place green moss over the base of the terrarium so you do not see soil or roots through the glass.

(2) Use contrasting foliage plants, some feathery, some stiff and smooth.

(3) Use different kinds of moss in shades from yellow-green to blue-green and gray-green.

(4) Arrange your material so that you cannot see all at a glance but must turn it, or move around it to observe everything.

(5) Plan for varying heights in the planting.

(6) Have a path. Discovering a path is as exciting in a terrarium as in life.

We add then our private rules: *Nothing* artificial, no colored stones, no Japanese pagodas, bridges, or figurines. We try to make our terrarium plantings resemble natural woodland.

When you have arranged all to your liking, spray the little scene with water at room temperature and put on a cover. Then pause to admire. The sparkling drops of water on the plants add enchantment.

WILD FLOWERS TO GROW

One year, a few weeks before Christmas, in one afternoon I made ten terrarium plantings in different sizes of brandy snifters. It was my favorite gift that year, and the reception was warm and enthusiastic.

PLACEMENT

The ideal place to keep a terrarium where it will thrive and grow all winter is *touching the glass at a north window with good light*. If the terrarium glass touches the window glass, it absorbs coolness from outdoors and the plants keep fresh and green. Every day or so lift the top for a few moments. Put your hand in and enjoy the pleasant tropical atmosphere, while the plants are getting necessary fresh air. Sprinkle lightly every week if the planting seems dry—but only lightly. *Never* let water appear at the bottom of the container. *Never* let the planting become soggy, and *never* let the sun shine on your terrarium or in two days it will mold. If you make terrariums for Christmas presents, start work a week or two in advance and keep the finished terrariums in a cool room with the glass touching the panes of a north window. They will then be fresh and lovely for Christmas Eve and delivery time.

Part III

WILD FLOWERS TO PROTECT

. . . in Wildness is the preservation of the World.
—HENRY DAVID THOREAU

13. Conservation and Common Sense

Conservation is the use of natural resources in ways that are wise—ways that result in the greatest good for the largest number of people for the longest time. Today, to this end, countless successful efforts are being made throughout the country by the government, communities large and small, garden clubs, and individuals.*

In Tryon, North Carolina there used to be a lovely custom. On the first warm spring days, mountain women, down from their cabins, stood at the corners on Main Street selling budding branches, quince, pear, peach, apple. They also sold small bunches of fragrant Trailing Arbutus. But each year they had to go farther and farther up the wooded slopes to find this gradually vanishing plant.

In Connecticut last year a six-year-old brought her

* I am greatly indebted to Alice Harvey Hubbard for her book *This Land of Ours,* published by the Macmillan Company. Mrs. Hubbard gives a very lively account of what has been done as well as a blueprint of what can be done. Her book has been the source of much of the information in these chapters on conservation.

mother a birthday bunch of pink Lady's-Slippers discovered in nearby woods. In California a whole mountainside of wild blue Lupine was bulldozed off to make room
for a hundred houses. In Iowa a dangerous curve was
taken out of a road and a thousand Bloodroot plants were
destroyed.

Along the Connecticut coast a marsh is being filled in
to create a parking lot for a nearby beach. On the Gover-
nor's desk lies a letter from a little boy—a childish scrawl
and somewhat grubby. It says, "My dog and me we like
to walk in the marsh and play in the shallow pools where
baby fish live. Sometimes my little sister comes. She
picks cattails and those big pink flowers. They are dump-
ing sand on the cattails and flowers, and I can't find any-
more baby fish, please tell them to stop. We like to play
there, me and my sister."

Who could blame the mountain women in Tryon?
Their children needed shoes for school. Love prompts the
little girl to pick flowers for her mother's birthday. Obviously houses must be built, dangerous curves elimi-
nated, and bathers must park. Each one of these projects
answers a need, but add them to countless similar in-
stances, and you realize that our wilderness areas are
rapidly diminishing.

198

CONSERVATION AND COMMON SENSE

OUR HERITAGE

All across the country from the east coast to the west are sections that stir us to wonder. Have you ever driven through the rolling hills of Missouri when fresh new green was everywhere? The Redbud was in flower, and mingled with it drifts of snowy Dogwood, and beneath them carpets of Spring Beauty. Springtime in Texas is vistas of Blue Bonnets bringing earth and sky together while among them rises the flaming Indian Paintbrush. High in the Colorado Mountains native Blue Columbine dances in sunlight and shadow. On the Atlantic Coast brilliant Goldenrod blows along the sandy beaches.

The more you explore this country, the more you value its floral wealth. What can we do about this treasure of wild beauty so dangerously threatened by the hand of man?

Step one is understanding what lies back of the whole idea of conservation, the idea of preserving as well as developing our natural resources. Marshes are important to the small boy and his sister. All wilderness is vital to us personally. Whether we are aware of it or not, we need intervals of woods and meadows, beaches and marshes. This nation needs more tranquility and places that foster it. Camping trips, fishing, riding, hiking, or just walking up a nearby gorge contribute to health, serenity, and general well-being. "A leaven of wildness is necessary for the health of the human spirit, a truth we seem to have forgotten in our headlong rush to control all nature," writes Eliot Porter. And Ralph Waldo Emerson said, "In the woods we return to reason and faith."

MARSHES AND SWAMPS

The core of the idea of conservation is that the land also requires for its own preservation these marshes, forests, and meadows.

A marsh is a fine demonstration of how nature takes care of her own. A stretch of wetland along the coast is a buffer that helps protect the land from hurricane seas. Cattails and Sea Lavender thrive, and Alder produces bright red berries for the nesting shore birds and the migrating flocks that pause to rest.

A marsh is vital to fish life in the surrounding waters. In shallows, fish hatch and are later caught and marketed. And, of course, great numbers escape to the sea and return the next spring to spawn. The parking lot that eliminates the marsh to increase the town treasury destroys flowers and wild life and affects the fishing industry of the neighborhood.

CONSERVATION AND COMMON SENSE

Can't the fish go somewhere else? Perhaps, but already a large percentage of our Atlantic shoreline and tidal wetlands have been abolished. We need all the rest.

Inland swamps are as important to the balance of nature as the coastline. Aside from its lovely wildlings, an inland swamp helps maintain the water table. As pavements spread over square miles of ground in growing towns and cities, the earth has an even greater need of marshes to offset them. In the city, water runs along gutters into culverts, and the soil gets little or none of it. But in marsh areas, rainfall is absorbed. A swamp, like a sponge, gathers water, stores it, and later lets it seep down into the underground reservoir.

THE FORESTS

In this country one third of our total land is forest. We admire the majesty of our trees, the sweeps of Wild Ginger, Hepatica, Bloodroot, and Trillium. Woodlands play a vital role in the scheme of conservation. Under trees snow lingers; melting slowly, it feeds springs and rivers over a long period of time. Trees break the rainfall, and layers of leaves on the ground absorb the drops. The forest floor is also a sponge. Water seeps down into the friable soil and the excess runs into streams and springs. Since it loses water gradually, a forest helps prevent flood and erosion. The worst erosion takes place where too many trees have been cleared. Undeveloped ridgeland, especially if tree-covered, is the very best sponge of all.

What does one less swamp, one less forest, or one more city matter in a country as large as ours? What does one more bouquet of Arbutus sold on the streets of Tryon matter? Are these *really* important?

When a storm comes, sweeping small craft out to sea, ripping off roofs and felling trees, we immediately see the damage. Individuals and communities staunchly meet these crises. But in the matter of conservation the changes brought about are seldom dramatic and not so noticeable. The problems are only evinced as a gradual whittling away. One must go higher in the mountains for the Arbutus. "There aren't so many blue Gentians as when I was young," an older woman will say.

PROGRESS AND CONSERVATION

There are two ways to approach the problem of progress versus conservation. You can sputter and fume and resist every new house and highway in your community, or you can go along with progress in an enlightened and constructive way, first learning yourself, next awakening the interest of others in the idea of conservation and what each of us can do to promote it.

The more you delve into the subject the less you think of nature "as a mere backdrop for man who is Divine," as Ian McHarg expressed it at the Annual Connecticut Conservation Conference. Mr. McHarg added, "Man may be Divine, but so are some other things, and nature isn't just stuff!"

Dr. Walter Lowdermilk, the famous conservationist, wrote that unless we took drastic steps there was danger of the fields becoming sterile and our descendants perishing. To this end he devised an Eleventh Commandment. Here is part of it:

"Thou shalt inherit the Holy Earth as a faithful steward, conserving its resources and productivity from generation to generation. Thou shalt safeguard thy fields from soil erosion, thy living waters from drying up, thy forests from desolation, and protect thy herds that thy descendants may have abundance forever. . . ."

Government agencies are increasingly aware of the conservation needs of the states and the country. Certain communities and townships are planning with greater wisdom in regard to land needs. More often these days they employ scientific knowledge of land requirements and water tables when planning highways and housing developments. Thought is given to conservation whenever industry moves in. In a few townships whenever there is new construction, balancing areas of undeveloped land for wild life and native flora are set aside.

Knowledge is spreading. It should spread farther, and we can all help. Find out about national conservation goals and your local situation and needs. As a member of a community with Women's Clubs and Garden Clubs, you have the opportunity to arouse group enthusiasm. Shared responsibility within clubs, within townships and communities can generate a tremendous force for constructive action.

14. What Communities and Garden Clubs are Doing

All over the country the activities of communities and garden clubs are bearing fruit. What imagination, energy, single-mindedness, and persistence these groups demonstrate.

In Ohio, when a plan for a new turnpike threatened a large and beautiful growth of Dogwood, interested citizens—spurred on by garden club members—turned out on a day designated with shovels. Boy Scouts and high school students pitched in, and together they moved every tree. Local schools, churches, public buildings, private residences, and the town pump each received a share of the rescued trees.

In Westport, Connecticut, garden club members planted Dogwood trees along rural roads. Today, thanks to them, you drive through a fairyland of bloom each May.

At one time, townships considered a swamp something to fill in. Today a different point of view prevails. Outside Rochester, New York, lies Bergen Swamp. Some years ago one of the residents, Mrs. Walter B. Slifer, saw the great possibilities of this area. Her enthusiasm led to the formation of the Bergen Swamp Preservation Society which purchased several hundred acres. White and yellow Lady's-Slippers thrive in the area along with Azaleas and the rather rare Lizard's-Tail. Warblers sing, the great horned owl and the whippoorwill preside. In this world apart, visitors find peace and beauty as well as a living laboratory for scientific study. Students of all ages come to learn and to appreciate. The Society also prepared a handsomely illustrated booklet, "Swamp Treasure," to enlighten people of the vicinity about the importance of swamps.

REDWOOD STORY

A little over forty years ago a big campaign was launched in California to save the Redwoods. As John Muir, an ardent pleader in their behalf, said, "We are not building this country of ours for a day, it is to last through the ages." Due to him and to the determination of other citizens, great strides were made. Ninety percent of the Sierra Redwoods (*Sequoia gigantea*) and a proportion of the Coastal Redwoods (*Sequoia sempervirens*) are now protected in state and national parks, or national forests where the great brown trunks rise a hundred feet or so above carpets of Ferns and flowers. These parks are places of beauty and wonder to visit, to drive through, or to camp in.

A hundred-acre sanctuary called Bowman's Hill Wild Flower Preserve stands today on the Pennsylvania side of the Delaware where General Washington camped before the Battle of Trenton. This sanctuary grew out of a casual conversation. One afternoon in 1933, Mrs. Henry Parry was setting out Daffodil bulbs when a friend from the Department of Forests came by. They talked of the beauty of a particular wooded area and means of protecting it. Garden clubs and other organizations got behind their idea and Bowman's Hill Preserve was thus created.

In Washington, Connecticut, seventy-seven years ago a certain man saved his money to build a house. Then he learned that the land, including what had long been known as Steep Rock above the Shepaug River, had been bought by a lumber company to timber off. With his savings, this farsighted, selfless man purchased 186 acres, including Steep Rock, to conserve this unique area for a natural park. In 1925, he deeded it to Trustees, and since that time other citizens have donated additional parcels to enlarge this reservation to a total of more than 1200 acres. The area is maintained by the Board of Trustees with contributions from over a hundred local residents. There are now miles of bridle trails and nature walks through wooded glades on both sides of the river. There are no buildings on either bank for more than four miles. And, incidentally, the man did build his house after a further period of saving.

GROUP PROJECTS

A new idea in development planning is the Cluster System. Each house is allotted a small garden and private yard, all clustered in one section of the land tract. The remaining open spaces and woodland are for everyone to enjoy.

Many such examples throughout the country reveal the average American's love of wilderness and his desire to conserve it. The present accomplishment is an inspiration, and there are many further opportunities. At the edge of nearly all townships lie tracts of land with little or no real estate value. A village or club group could buy and convert such acreage into a sanctuary or leave it in wildness. Several towns could combine and purchase adjoining areas. In some places this is already being done.

Group projects involve saving marshes; saving flood plains as a protection for land behind them; saving valleys and wooded hilltops; purifying rivers and streams, especially near factories. Most conservationists groan when factories try to come into their community, but industry often cooperates magnificently with nature though sometimes unwittingly. Along the Connecticut River recently, mysterious plants from other parts of the world were discovered, varieties never before seen in the vicinity. Botanists followed the river searching for the source of the flowers. They discovered a factory where shipments of ancient rubber overshoes from all over the world arrived to be processed. Seeds clinging to mud-caked soles had found new earth in which to sprout.

Shoes have helped before to spread seed. Years ago a Roman soldier crossed the Channel to England and flopped on the ground to rest. He tossed his muddy boots into a ditch. Next year blossoms new to Britain sprang up from those clods of Gallic mire for nature is incredibly ingenious at spreading seed. On Long Island, Musk Thistles, native to Europe, now thrive near the site of the 1939 World's Fair; doubtless they came over in some packing material. The European Mullein probably arrived here by some such devious route. English plant-hunters took this back to naturalize in Britain, calling it the American Velvet Plant.

WILD FLOWERS TO PROTECT

In conservation much work has already been done, and every new community or garden club project adds momentum. Furthermore, almost every one of these activities has been sparked by the enthusiasm of a single individual.

15. What You Can Do

Conservation needs the effort of every individual, the work of each of us. Perhaps you are not a joiner, not even a garden club member. You may have almost no time for town affairs. But still you appreciate nature and wild flowers. What can you do? You can grow them.

In your own garden, large or small, find a place for wild flowers. If you have an acre you can grow multitudes. Propagate varieties that are scarce. Robert Lemon, the famous author, has devoted almost the whole of his Connecticut garden to wild flowers. He planted them where they would flourish and many sorts, nearly extinct, are now thriving there.

If there is a damp or boggy place on your land, build a pond. The supervisor of your soil conservation district will send a Soil Conservation Service scientist to check. If the place is suitable, his engineers will design a dam for you. Federal and state aid in almost every state will pay up to half the cost of this improvement. Your mosquito-infested bog can become a charming pond, perhaps with a little island where Canada geese may nest. Wild ducks will come. Marsh Marigolds, Wild Calla, Water Lilies, Pickerelweed, and dozens of other water-loving plants will thrive in your pond. And in winter, young folks can skate there. Thus you enhance your property and enrich your family life while preserving the local water table and doing the cause of conservation a great service.

Today the World

Do you think of your garden as ending at the edge of your property?

Imagine for a moment that your backyard is the whole United States, for in a way it is since your tax money keeps up national parks and preserves national forests. Considering the whole country as your garden (and happily one that *you* need not cultivate) adds a new dimension to your horticultural enthusiasm. This thought may lead you to emulate the women of the Texas garden club who scatter wild flower seeds in their neighborhoods. If you know of a flourishing stand of Day Lilies, Black-eyed Susans, Gentians, or Dutchman's-Breeches, return later in the season to harvest the seeds. Take note of where the plants grow and sow the seed in similar conditions.

The Johnny Appleseed method is still rewarding. Go one mile with nature and she goes three with you. A seed in the right place today becomes a dozen plants in a few years.

Light One Candle

Nature has a staunch ally in the Woodbury-Southbury section of Connecticut where George Bennett, a postman for thirty years, steadily has aided the cause of conservation. Mrs. Hubbard tells us about him. "Would you like some Multiflora Rose roots for that eroding bank?" he asks as he delivers the mail. "I have a few here in the car. In fact, I will help you plant them." Thus on George Bennett's route the arrival of the mail means more than letters and through his personal conservation crusade, he sees his garden extending far beyond his own picket fence to include the fifty-one thousand or so acres that border his route.

In the Black Hills of South Dakota, yellow Lady's-Slippers were becoming rare when Mr. J. M. Atkinson of Rapid City sought out the few remaining sweeps of these flowers, noted their sites, gathered the ripened seed, and planted them in suitable locations. Returning a few springs later he found several valleys rich with the yellow flowers. Thanks to Mr. Atkinson the golden Lady's-Slippers of the Black Hills may someday be as plentiful as they once were.

Suppose you live in a city, what can you do? Three women in a Philadelphia slum area decided to do something about a trash-filled lot behind a tall fence. They worked secretly after dark. Slipping through the back alleys with baskets in three months they had cleared away the rubble. Then plant by plant, they created a flourishing garden within the fence. One morning at dawn they took away the fence. A man of the neighborhood was so moved by the sight of the flowers that he built a picket fence to protect them. At Christmas that first year, and every year since, a tall evergreen is set up in the center and decorated by neighbors who gather around it to sing carols on Christmas Eve.

When you begin thinking about conservation, your attitude toward crops alters. No longer do you consider the soil in your vegetable garden as something into which you put a seed in April and out of which you take a carrot in July. Your point of view about a handful of soil changes. You see it as productive earth teaming with beneficent bacteria—no wonder it feels alive and smells good.

Your sense of the land changes too. In that range of hills across the meadow, you sense the sap rising in the trees in spring and draining down into the earth again in the fall. An awareness of nature's purpose quickens in you. This hill has a role to play; this land is a friendly force, an ally to be protected.

Theodore Roosevelt, a great conservationist, wrote, "Do what you can where you are, with what you've got." You may have room for only a dozen Trillium in your backyard, or you may have space for a thousand on your country acres. Either way you can do something worthwhile.

Once you enter this exciting field of conservation you find that one idea begets another. From planting wild flowers to building ponds, each single action, small in itself, is another brick in place. The most solid walls are no more than many once-separate bricks.

NINE GUIDES FOR
WILD FLOWER ENTHUSIASTS

1. Learn what flowers are on your state conservation list.
2. Obey conservation laws. Do not pick flowers or other plant material that is prohibited.
3. Grow as many native plants on your own place as you can. Broadcast as much seed as possible.
4. Don't buy wild plants from dealers unless you are sure they are nursery propagated and grown, not collected.

215

5. Don't buy bouquets of wild flowers if they have been gathered from open land, which they almost always have.

6. Cut off blossoms when you do pick; don't pull them and so risk injuring roots. Leave some stems with leaves on the plant.

7. Gather only a few flowers from any one plant. Let the rest go to seed.

8. Don't forbid a child to pick all wild flowers. Explain instead what may be picked and what may not, and why.

9. Be cautious about campfires and dropped matches. Fire destroys woodland and wild flowers, and also the humus in the soil which is of such great value in plant growth and water storage.

16. Some You Pick
and Some You Don't

Picking wild flowers is not a matter of *whether* but of *which*. Summer and fall flowers are particularly lovely in arrangements. The vivid blooms of seaside Goldenrod bring sunshine into the house on a cloudy day. Daisies and Black-eyed Susans combine cheerfully. Red Clover and Daisy Fleabane have a sweet scent. Queen Anne's Lace is among the best.

Picking Violets is one of the joys of spring, Forget-me-nots make delightful bouquets for bedside tables. The large white blossoms of Datura, floating in a bowl, spread their scent through your rooms.

With your conservation list in hand—or in mind—go forth with scissors and a basket, but pick with discretion. The beauty and fragrance of your wild flower bouquet will bring joy to your household for many days.

The plants listed below are on the conservation lists of many states, and they deserve our protection wherever we find them. Some state lists may include others that do not appear here. If you are in doubt about picking certain flowers or digging plants, do inquire through your local garden club or write to your State Conservation Chairman, in care of the National Council of State Garden Clubs, 4401 Magnolia Avenue, St. Louis 10, Missouri. Through these sources you can find out which plants are protected in your particular area.

NATIVE PLANTS TO PROTECT

American Brooklime, Speedwell—*Veronica americana*
White lily—*Nymphaea odorata*
Atamasco Lily—*Zephyranthes atamasco*
Azalea, Clammy, Swamp—*Rhododendron viscosum*
        Flame—   *calendulaceum*
        Pinxterbloom—   *nudiflorum*
        Rhodora—   *canadense*
        Western—   *occidentale*

Beach Clotbur—*Xanthium echinatum*
Beach Pea—*Lathyrus maritimus*
Bearberry—*Arctostaphylos uva-ursi*
Bellwort—*Uvularia sessilifolia*
Bird's-Foot Violet—*Viola pedata*
Bittersweet—*Celastrus scandens*
Black Alder, Winterberry—*Ilex verticillata*
Bloodroot—*Sanguinaria canadensis*
Blue Cohosh—*Caulophyllum thalictroides*
Blue-eyed Grass—*Sisyrinchium angustifolium*
Blunt-leaved Milkweed—*Asciepias amplexicaulis*

SOME YOU PICK AND SOME YOU DON'T

Bottle or Closed Gentian—*Gentiana andrewsi*
Bunchberry—*Cornus canadensis*
Butterfly Weed—*Asclepias tuberosa*

California Poppy—*Eschscholtzia californica*
Canada Lily, Yellow Meadow Lily—*Lilium canadense*
Canada Violet—*Viola canadensis*
Cardinal Flower, Red Lobelia—*Lobelia cardinalis*
Climbing Wild Cucumber—*Echinocystis lobata*
Columbine—*Aquilegia canadensis*
Common Thistle—*Cirsium lanceolatum*
Clubmoss and Running Pine—*Lycopodium* sp.

Devil's-Paintbrush, Canada Hawkweed—*Hieracium canadense*
Dog's-Tooth Violet, Fawn Lily—*Erythronium americanum*
Dogwood—*Cornus* sp.
Dragon's-Mouth—*Arethusa bulbosa*
Dutchman's-Breeches—*Dicentra cucullaria*

False Solomon's-Seal—*Smilacina racemosa*
Five-Finger—*Potentilla canadensis*
Flaming Sword, Ocotillo—*Fouquieria splendens*
Foamflower—*Tiarella cordifolia*
Fringe Tree—*Chionanthus virginica*
Fringed Gentian—*Gentiana crinita*
Fringed Orchis—*Habenaria* sp.

Goldthread—*Coptis trifolia*
Great Lobelia—*Lobelia siphilitica*
Great Solomon's-Seal—*Polygonatum commutatum*
Ground Cedar—*Lycopodium tristachyum*

219

WILD FLOWERS TO PROTECT

Hawthorn-*Crataegus* (native sp.)
Heartleaf, Twayblade—*Listera cordata*
Hedge Bindweed—*Convolvulus sepium*
Hempweed Vine, Boneset—*Mikania scandens*
Hepatica, Liverleaf—*Hepatica triloba*
Hobblebush—*Viburnum alnifolium*
Holly—*Ilex* sp.

Indian Pipe—*Montropa uniflora*
Indian Poke, False or American White Hellebore—*Veratrum viride*

Jack-in-the-Pulpit—*Arisaema triphyllum*
Jacob's-Ladder—*Polemonium vanbruntiae*

Lady's-Slipper—*Cypripedium* sp.
Large Flowering Trillium—*Trillium grandiflorum,* also *T.* sp.
Large Purple-fringed Orchis—*Habenaria fimbriata*
  Sheep, Lambkill—*angustifolia*
Leather Flower—*Clematis ochroleuca*
Lupine—*Lupinus perennis*

Magnolia—*Magnolia* (native sp.)
Marsh Marigold—*Caltha palustris*
Marsh Trefoil, Buck Bean—*Menyanthes trifoliata*
May Apple, Wild Mandrake—*Podophyllum peltatum*
Moccasin Flower—*Cypripedium acaule*
Moss Pink—*Phlox subulata*

Nightshade—*Solanum dulcamara*

SOME YOU PICK AND SOME YOU DON'T

Partridgeberry, Twinberry—*Mitchella repens*
Partridge Pea—*Cassia chamaecrista*
Pasqueflower—*Anemone patens*
Pinesap, Beechdrops—*Monotropa hypopitys*
Pink Catchfly—*Silene pennsylvanica*
Pipissewa, Prince's Pine—*Chimaphila umbellata*
Pitcher Plant—*Sarracenia purpurea*

Rattlesnake Plantain—*Epipactis tesselata*
Redbud—*Cercis canadensis*
Rough-fruited Cinquefoil—*Potentilla recta*
Round-leaved Sundew—*Drosera rotundifolia*
Running Pine—*Lycopodium complanatum*

Shadbush, Shadblow—*Amelanchier canadensis*
Showy Orchis—*Orchis spectabilis*
Silverbell Tree—*Halesia* sp.
Slender Ladies'-Tresses—*Spiranthes gracilis*
Small-leaved Burdock—*Arctium minus*
Smilax, Greenbrier—*Smilax* (native sp.)
Solomon's-Seal—*Polygonatum biflorum*
Sourwood, Sorrel Tree—*Oxydendron arboreum*
Spicebush—*Benzoin aestivale*
Spring Beauty—*Claytonia virginica*
Squirrelcorn—*Dicentra canadensis*
Starflower—*Trientalis borealis*
Star Grass—*Hypoxis hirsuta*
Stewartia—*Stewartia* sp.
Strawberry Bush—*Euonymus americanus*
Swamp Rose Mallow—*Hibiscus moscheutos*
Sweet Bay—*Magnolia virginiana*

WILD FLOWERS TO PROTECT

Tall Meadow Rue—*Thalictrum polygamum*
Thimbleweed—*Anemone virginiana*
Toothwort, Crinkleroot—*Dentaria diphylla*
Trailing Arbutus, Mayflower—*Epigaea repens*
Trillium, Wake-Robin, Birthroot—*Trillium* sp.
Tulip Poplar—*Liriodendron tulipifera*
Turk's-Cap Lily—*Lilium superbum*
Turtlehead—*Chelone glabra*

Virginia Cowslip, Bluebells—*Mertensia virginica*

Water Hemlock, Spotted Cowbane—*Cicuta maculata*
Western Evening Primrose—*Anogra albicaulis*
White Water Lily—*Nymphaea odorata*
Wild Calla, Water Arum—*Calla palustris*
Wild Geranium, Cranesbill—*Geranium maculatum*
Wild Ginger—*Asarum canadense*
Wild Lily-of-the-Valley—*Maianthemum canadense*
Wintergreen, Checkerberry—*Gaultheria procumbens*
Witch Hazel—*Hamamelis virginiana*
Wood Anemone, Wind Flower—*Anemone quinquefolia*
Wood Lily—*Lilium philadelphicum*
Wood Sorrel—*Oxalis acetosella*

Yellow Jessamine—*Gelsemium sempervirens*
Yellow Mountain Saxifrage—*Leptasea aizoides*
Yellow Pond Lily, Spatterdock—*Nymphaea advena*
Yellow Violet—*Viola pubescens*
Yucca—*Hespero-Yucca whipplei*

Epilogue: Wild Flowers for All of You Everywhere

We have a great heritage beyond the reach of depression or inflation, moth or rust, a treasure not to be confined in a vault—one free to us all—our American wild flowers.

Every year this rich land burgeons with myriads of colors and forms. Along the Cape Cod beaches in June the fragrance of Rugosa Roses enchants you. In summer, California's rugged shores are golden with Poppies. Far-famed are the lovely furry-leaved Pasqueflowers of Minnesota's prairies, and the sweet Trailing Arbutus of the Smoky Mountains.

Great sweeps of wild flowers are not limited to spring. In August drifts of lavender Bee Balm scent the farm valleys of New York state, while the New England marshes are pink with meadowsweet. Purple Joe-Pye Weed borders the woods in many places. To end the season, dark purple Asters and bright Goldenrod paint the country

223

roads beneath flame-red and yellow maples. Somewhere wild flowers are always blooming.

Too often we overlook the familiar in our reach for a far star. We should not stop reaching, but we should sometimes pause to enjoy the beauty near at hand—sunlight on grass, raindrops on Fern fronds, cool running streams, a single Fringed Gentian on an October hilltop, blue as the sky above it.

In our busy concerns, we may overlook wild flowers pushing up through wet leaves with the first breath of spring, and going down to frost in the first cold. We are often so impressed by acres of drama, that we miss the less flamboyant charm of a patch of Trout Lilies or Milkweed seeds packed in a pod but ready to fly away on the breeze, and the crop of shiny orange Rugosa berries at the close of the season.

You may prefer drama by the acre, or enjoy it flower by flower at the streambank. All this may be new to you or a familiar story. In any case, I warmly welcome you to the world of wild flowers which I have found rich with joy and lasting rewards, where every season is fresh with new discovery.

Some Dealers in Native Plants

CLAUDE A. BARR
Smithwick, South Dakota

BAY STATE NURSERIES
North Abington, Massachusetts

WILL CURTIS
Garden in the Woods
South Sudbury, Massachusetts

EXETER WILD FLOWER GARDEN
Exeter, New Hampshire

FERNDALE NURSERIES
Askov, Minnesota

GARDENS OF THE BLUE RIDGE
E. C. Robbins
Ashford, North Carolina

GARDENSIDE NURSERIES
Shelburne, Vermont

WAKE ROBIN FARM
Route #1, Box 33,
Home, Pennsylvania

RUTH HARDY'S WILD FLOWER
NURSERY
U.S. Route #7
Falls Village, Connecticut

KNICKELBEIN'S WILD LIFE NURS-
ERIES
Jackson Drive Road
Route 5, Box 26
Oshkosh, Wisconsin

LOUNSBERRY GARDENS
Oakford, Illinois

PEARCE SEED CO.,
Moorestown, New Jersey

PUTNEY NURSERY CO.,
Putney, Vermont

VALLEY GARDENS
21301 Telegraph Road
Detroit, Michigan

VICKS WILD GARDENS
Narberth, Pennsylvania

Bibliography

Birdseye, Clarence and Eleanor G. *Growing Woodland Plants.* New York: Oxford University Press, 1951.

Fernald, Merritt Lyndon, ed. *Gray's Manual of Botany.* New York: American Book Company, 1950, Eighth Edition.

Gibbons, Euell. *Stalking the Wild Asparagus.* New York: David McKay Company, Inc., 1962.

Gottscho, Samuel H. *Wild Flowers.* New York: Dodd, Mead & Company, Inc., 1951.
  One hundred and three excellent photographs in full color, with one hundred and twenty-two black-and-whites, all by the author. Detailed guide to growing—and enjoying—wild flowers.

Hubbard, Alice Harvey. *This Land of Ours.* New York: The Macmillan Company, 1960.
  A fascinating study of conservation. What is being done all over the country, and what you can do.

Johnson, C. Pierpoint. *Our Useful Wild Flowers.* London: William Kent & Company, 1862.

Mathews, F. Schuyler. *Field Book of American Wild Flowers.* New York: G. P. Putnam's Sons, 1902.
  Old-fashioned, but fine book on identification of wild plants and flowers. Drawings in black and white and in color.

Taylor, Norman. *Wild Flower Gardening.* Princeton: D. Van Nostrand Company, Inc., 1955.

WILD FLOWER PRESERVES, TRAILS AND AREAS TO BE VISITED †

ARIZONA
Boyce Thompson Arboretum, Superior
Saguaro National Monument, near Tucson

CALIFORNIA
Coastal Route 1 from Los Angeles to Monterey (spring)**
Route 91 from Mountain Pass to Barstow
Route 66 to Santa Barbara and beyond
Muir Woods National Monument, 2 miles southwest of Mill Valley
*Point Lobos State Park, near Carmel (May and June)
Torrey Pines Preserve, La Jolla
*Yosemite National Park (after July 15)

COLORADO
Cheyenne Mountain Nature Preserve, Colorado Springs

*Rocky Mountain National Parks, Estes Park

CONNECTICUT
Fairchild Wild Flower Sanctuary, Greenwich
Hubbard Park Sanctuary, Meriden
Marsh Botanical Garden, Yale University, New Haven
Litchfield Wild Flower Sanctuary, Litchfield
New Canaan Sanctuary, New Canaan
Pootatuck State Forest Nature Trail, New Fairfield

DISTRICT OF COLUMBIA
*Fern Valley Trail, National Arboretum, near Washington

FLORIDA
Everglades State Park, Homestead
Tamiami Trail, Miami to Ft. Myers

† Reprinted from *Plants & Gardens,* Brooklyn Botanic Garden Record, Spring 1962, courtesy of the Brooklyn Botanic Garden.

* Areas marked with an asterisk have descriptive booklets. In addition, all Richfield gas stations in California, Oregon and Washington distribute colored wildflower booklets containing maps.

** Dates given indicate the seasons of outstanding displays.

Route 1, south of Jacksonville

Routes 19 and 98, Tampa to Pensacola and Jacksonville west (spring)

GEORGIA
Callaway Garden, Pine Mountain Preserve, Hamilton

ILLINOIS
Morton Arboretum, Lisle

INDIANA
*Indiana Botanical Garden, Hammond

MAINE
Baxter State Park, near Millinocket (June)
*Acadia National Park, Bar Harbor

MARYLAND
Cylburn Wild Flower Preserve, Baltimore

MASSACHUSETTS
Bartholomew's Cobble, south of Sheffield

MINNESOTA
Eloise Butler Wild Flower Garden, Wirth Park, Minneapolis

MISSISSIPPI
Route 90, across Mississippi and Louisiana (April)

MISSOURI
Missouri Botanical Garden Arboretum, Gray's Summit
Tucker Prairie, Route 40, East of Columbia

MONTANA
Route 12, from Yellowstone National Park east (July)
*Glacier National Park (open after July 15)

NEW HAMPSHIRE
Alpine Garden, Mt. Washington (late June and early July)
Lost River Nature Reservations, Kingman Notch, North Woodstock (after June 15)

NEW JERSEY
Batsto Nature Area, Wharton Tract, Greenbrook, Egg Harbor City
Bennett Bog Sanctuary, three miles north of Cape May City
Jockey Hollow Wild Flower Preserve, Morristown
Lucine L. Lorrimer Sanctuary, Franklin Lakes

228

Mettler's Woods, near East Millstone

Watchung Reservation, Westfield

NEW YORK

Bergen Swamp, Genessee County

Wild Flower Garden, Brooklyn Botanic Garden, Brooklyn

Wild Flower Garden, The New York Botanical Garden, Bronx Park

Pound Ridge Reservation, Cross River

Westmoreland Sanctuary, Mt. Kisco

NORTH CAROLINA

Holly Refuge, near Burgau (late May)

Pearson Falls Wild Flower Sanctuary, Tryon

OHIO

Nature Trails and Museum, Cleveland Park System, Cleveland

Harriet Keeler Memorial Woods Reservation, near Breckville

Madden Park, Route 6, Dayton

North Chagrin Nature Trail, between Mayfield and Chardon Road, Cleveland

Fine Arts Garden, Plant Sanctuary, Euclid Ave. and East Boulevard, Cleveland

Pine Hill Arboretum, near West Fairview

Shaker Wild Flower Preserve, Cleveland

OREGON

*Crater Lake National Park, near Medford (after July 1-15)

Macleary Park Native Plant Sanctuary, Cornell Rd. via N.W. Lovejoy at city limit, Portland

Route 50, from Rhododendron to Government Camp (mid-June)

Route 35 north, slopes of Mt. Hood (mid-June)

PENNSYLVANIA

*Bowman's Hill State Wild Flower Preserve, Washington Crossing

Tinicum Sanctuary, Philadelphia

Powdermill Nature Reserve, Westmoreland County

Ohio Pyle Preserve, Fayette County

Tyler Arboretum, Lima

TENNESSEE

Elise Chapin Wildlife Sanctuary, near Chattanooga

Shelby County Forest, Bird and
Plant Sanctuary, 15 miles north
of Memphis
*Great Smoky Mountains National Park, Gatlinburg

TEXAS
*Big Bend National Park
Little Thicket Nature Sanctuary,
Evergreen

UTAH
Zion National Park

VERMONT
Long Trail Lodge and Nature
Trail, Sherbourne Pass (Green
Mountains), 10 miles east of
Rutland

VIRGINIA
Conway Robinson Memorial
Forest, Gainesville
*Blue Ridge Parkway, from Rockfish Gap near Afton, Va. to
Asheville, N.C.

Jacksonville Memorial Wild
Flower Preserve, Chancellorsville
Pilgrim Rest Sanctuary and Nature Trail, adjoining Woodland
Cemetery, Norfolk
*Shenandoah National Park,
Front Royal to Rockfish Gap
(near Afton)

WASHINGTON
*Olympic National Park (after
July 15)
*Mt. Rainier National Park (after
July 15)

WEST VIRGINIA
Oglebay Park, five miles from
Wheeling on U.S. Route 250

WISCONSIN
University of Wisconsin Arboretum, near Madison

WYOMING
*Yellowstone National Park

Index

(References are to page numbers except where a plate number is given (Pl. 1:1) in italics. In these cases the individual flowers are described on the page facing the color plate. The numbers after the italicized *Pl.* indicate the number of the plate and the illustration number.)

INDEX

232

INDEX